COLUMBUS

500 YEARS

The World Book of

# AMERICA'S HERITAGE

belongs to the library of:

# The World Book of
# AMERICA'S HERITAGE

The Peoples, Traditions,
and Aspirations
That Shaped North America

World Book, Inc.
a Scott Fetzer company
Chicago   London   Sydney   Toronto

# STAFF

**Publisher**
William H. Nault

**President**
Tom Murphy

**Editorial**

**Executive editor**
Dominic J. Miccolis

**Associate editor**
Maureen Mostyn Liebenson

**Senior editors**
Karen Zack Ingebretsen
Lisa Klobuchar

**Editor**
Kathleen Manatt

**Copy editor**
Irene Keller

**Researcher**
Vicki Musial

**Permissions editor**
Janet T. Peterson

**Writer**
James I. Clark

**Art**

**Art director**
Roberta Dimmer

**Senior editorial artist**
Deirdre Wroblewski

**Designers**
Brenda Tropinski
Chestnut House

**Production**
Donna Cook
Linda Kinnaman
Penelope Nichols
Sally Wayland

**Photography**

**Photography director**
John S. Marshall

**Photographs editors**
Geralyn A. Swietek
Julie Laffin
Katherine Nolan

**Product Production**

**Manufacturing director**
Sandra Van den Broucke

**Manufacturing assistant manager**
Eva Bostedor

**Pre-press services director**
Jerry Stack

**Senior production manager**
Randi Park

**Production manager**
Joann Seastrom

**Proofreaders**
Carolyn Crabtree
Anne Dillon
Marguerite Hoye
Daniel J. Marotta
Peter Shrock
Arlene Walters

## Consultants

Carol Berkin
Professor of History
Baruch College and CUNY
Graduate Center
New York, New York

Amina Dickerson
Director
Elizabeth Cheney Center for
Education and Public Programs
Chicago Historical Society
Chicago, Illinois

Philip Lax
President
Ellis Island Restoration
Commission
New York, New York

Copyright © 1991
World Book, Inc.
525 W. Monroe Street
Chicago, Illinois 60661

Printed in the United States of America.
ISBN 0-7166-3239-x
Library of Congress Catalog Card No. 91-65695

# PREFACE

*The World Book of America's Heritage* celebrates the rich diversity of people who proudly call themselves Americans. These books tell the powerful stories of groups and individuals who struggled to make better lives for themselves and their descendants.

Using a chronological format, the books present all the various groups of Americans, beginning with the earliest immigrants, who came across the Bering Strait from Asia many thousands of years ago. Volume 1 presents the people who arrived before 1800—the Indians, European explorers, Pilgrims, colonists, Loyalists, and Patriots. The book also sensitively portrays the plight of those unwilling immigrants, the Africans who were brought to the Western Hemisphere as slaves.

Volume 2 tells the lively story of the westward movement and the growth of America as a nation as the result of the Northwest Ordinance, the Louisiana Purchase, and the Mexican Cession. The book highlights the immigrants who came through Ellis Island and tells how that historic place is being restored and preserved today. The volume continues with events in the 20th century, including the appearance of new immigrant groups and the effects all groups have on one another.

Through the use of lavish illustrations and the words of the immigrants themselves, the reader can get the full impact of what it meant to be an American at different times in history. Maps also help point out where major events took place.

*The World Book of America's Heritage* also carefully explores the darker side of immigration through discussions of racial prejudice, discriminatory laws, and the sometimes-violent confrontations that have occurred between groups or individuals.

A number of feature pages in each volume are also devoted to interesting historical sites, special world events, or noteworthy people. These include New Salem, Ill., the development of sailing ships, and the American expatriates. Also highlighted in special sections are the immigration movements to Canada, Hawaii, and Alaska.

*The World Book of America's Heritage* presents the pageant of America's people—their joys and sorrows, their successes and failures. Here, in words and pictures, are the stories of those who have become known as Americans.

# CONTENTS

## Book One

# Book Two

In 1803, the United States bought from France the land that came to be known as the Louisiana Purchase. The city of New Orleans was part of the purchase, and this painting shows the city in that year. The Louisiana Purchase was the most important event of President Thomas Jefferson's first Administration, since it doubled the area of the United States. The price paid was about $15 million.

# PART 6: THE IMMIGRANT FLOW CONTINUES

EVERY THING PROSPERS

After slowing down during the war years, immigration picked up again, with 5 million newcomers arriving in America between 1815 and 1860. Immigrants in this period witnessed an outburst of nativism that lasted until slavery replaced it as an important issue in American life. In the meantime, pioneers settled the Old Northwest and the South, despite strong Native American resistance.

*Covered wagons carried thousands of pioneers westward, often to land where various Indian tribes lived. Sometimes, the pioneers traveled in peace. At other times, there were great battles with the Indians.*

# CHAPTER 16: INTERNAL MIGRATION: THE TREK BEGINS

Richard Henderson made no small plans. He saw himself as the creator and sole real estate broker of a vast empire beyond the Appalachian Mountains. He aimed to acquire millions of acres of Indian land and sell it piece by piece at a tidy profit to pioneers from North Carolina and other colonies, as well as to immigrants who had just arrived.

Shawnee chief Tecumseh, shown opposite, violently opposed the coming of the settlers. A gifted orator, he traveled widely and spoke often to other Indian tribes to gain supporters for his beliefs. Tecumseh joined forces with the British against the Americans in the War of 1812. He was killed in one of the battles.

Despite the uprisings, the settlers kept coming. One was Daniel Boone, shown here leading a group of settlers through the Cumberland Gap into Kentucky. Boone sometimes worked for Richard Henderson of North Carolina. Another famous early settler was Jean Baptiste Point Du Sable, a black pioneer. He was the first known settler to build a house and open a trading post in what later became Chicago, Illinois.

In 1775, Richard Henderson formed the Transylvania Company and journeyed west with a number of settlers to purchase land from the Indians. Henderson and his party met with representatives from several tribes at Sycamore Shoals on the bank of the Wautauga River in eastern Tennessee.

Most of the Indians attending were willing to exchange land for trade goods. However, there were some dissenters. Dragging Canoe, a Chickamauga, said that Indian had fought Indian over that land for generations. It had always been a bloody ground and would continue to be. In effect, he was warning the settlers that they were courting trouble.

In the end, Henderson got his land, some 32,000 square miles (83,000 square kilometers), which included a good part of both Kentucky and Tennessee. The Indians got beads, cloth, kettles, and knives.

185

*One of the most famous immigrants to America in the early 1800's was John James Audubon. A painter and naturalist, he was born in Haiti and raised in France. In 1803, his father sent him to America to escape conscription into the armies of Napoleon. For most of the next 17 years, Audubon was a business failure. With no other prospects, he decided to try publishing books of his bird pictures.*

As Henderson and his group moved into Kentucky in April 1775 along the Wilderness Road, they met other whites retreating from the area. Shawnee warriors had once more turned the land into a battleground. In his diary, Henderson wrote:

> Met about 40 persons returning from the Caintucky. Acct. of the Late Murder by the Indians could prevail on one only to return. Several Virginians who were with us returned to Virginia.

Encouraged by the British—who had occupied Detroit and other Western forts—and aided by British supplies and guns, Miami, Wyandot, Shawnee, and other Indians repeatedly raided Kentucky settlements and lonely frontier cabins. They left behind blackened ruins and many corpses, all missing a patch of hair and scalp—Indian tokens of victory.

Despite hardships and dangers, whites kept moving into Kentucky, but this migration proved of no bene-fit to Richard Henderson. According to the original charter establishing the Virginia colony, the land Henderson had bought belonged to Virginia, and Kentucky settlers petitioned the Virginia government to disallow Henderson's claim. Eventually, Virginia permitted Henderson to keep 200,000 acres (80,000 hectares) in return for his efforts in opening Kentucky to settlement, but the most he ever realized was 10 cents an acre (0.4 hectare).

In 1776, Kentucky became a county of Virginia, and by the end of the Revolutionary War it had been secured for the settlers. In 1792, Kentucky became the 15th state in the Union.

Settlers moving into Tennessee ignored Henderson's claims just as those in Kentucky did. They also met resistance from Cherokee, Chickasaw, and other tribes determined to keep whites out. The pioneers per-

another boy joined the family. Samuel named him Jefferson, after the President of the United States.

In 1810, after hearing about good cotton land to the south, the family and their slaves moved some 800 miles (1,280 kilometers) to an area that later became part of the state of Mississippi.

Jefferson Davis attended a log-cabin school near his home and then, for two years, a Roman Catholic school back in Kentucky. At age 16, he went to West Point to learn to be a soldier.

Nearly 200 years earlier, in 1637, a weaver named Samuel Lincoln had left Hingham, England, to settle in Hingham, Mass. His descendants, like those of John Davis, kept moving too—to New Jersey, Pennsylvania, and the back country of Virginia. The first Abraham Lincoln was born in Virginia in the 1700's. He married Bathsheba Herring, and they had three sons—Mordecai, Josiah, and Thomas—and two daughters—Nancy and Mary. From his friend Daniel Boone, Abraham Lincoln learned about rich land in Kentucky, selling then for 40 cents per acre (0.4 hectare), and he moved his family there in 1782. In 1786, a Shawnee killed him.

The youngest son, Thomas Lincoln, lacking an education and scarcely able to write his own name, worked as a farm hand in his youth, but became a carpenter later on. In 1806, at age 28, he married Nancy Hanks at Beech Fork in Washington County, Kentucky. Thomas then settled down—but not for long.

Living first in a small log cabin in Elizabethtown—where a daughter, Sarah, was born in 1807—the Lincolns moved in 1808 to Hodgen's Mill. There Thomas made a down payment on some land. In February 1809, a son was born, and the Lincolns named him Abraham, after his grandfather. Trouble with the title to the land caused the family to move again—this time across the Ohio into

*John James Audubon traveled through Kentucky and Louisiana, at much the same time the Davis family did, painting many pictures of the birds he saw. In 1826, Audubon went to England with his pictures, such as this one, which shows two pintail ducks. It was painted in New Orleans in February 1822. Audubon's pictures were an instant success, and by 1835, he was an international celebrity.*

sisted, however, and slowly made the land their own. In 1796, Tennessee entered the Union as the 16th state.

**T**wo Families. For many families moving west, Kentucky was a fork in the road. From there some pioneers moved south to Tennessee, Alabama, and Mississippi, while others traveled north to land across the Ohio River.

John Davis was an immigrant who arrived in Delaware from Wales in the 1660's. Samuel Davis, one of John's descendants, fought the British in South Carolina during the Revolutionary War. In 1793—with his wife, three boys, two girls, and a few slaves—Samuel Davis crossed the mountains into Kentucky. There the Davis family grew corn, wheat, and tobacco and raised horses. Four more girls were born, and on June 3, 1808,

# THE NORTHWEST TERRITORY

Mississippi River

Northwest Territory
1787

Ohio River

Not everyone who went to the Northwest Territory liked what they found, as this 1819 book, *Tour to Ohio*, explains.

WESTERN EMIGRATION.

JOURNAL

OF

DOCTOR JEREMIAH SMIPLETON's

TOUR TO OHIO.

CONTAINING
An account of the numerous difficulties, Hair-breadth Escapes, Mortifications and Privations, which the Doctor and his family experienced on their Journey from Maine, to the 'Land of Promise,' and during a residence of three years in that highly extolled country.

BY H. TRUMBULL.

*Nulli Fides Frontis.*

BOSTON--PRINTED BY S. SEWALL.

Early pioneers to the Northwest Territory sometimes lived near garrisons, such as this one, as protection against unfriendly Indians.

Indiana. In December 1816, the Lincolns settled at Pigeon Creek. Two years later, Nancy Lincoln died, and in 1819 Thomas married again—this time to a widow with three children.

Indiana was not to be the Lincolns' final place of residence, however. Thomas heard about richer soil farther west, in Illinois in the Northwest Territory. So in 1830, the family set out in wagons drawn by oxen for yet another new home.

Settling the Old Northwest. In 1787, the Congress had passed a remarkable piece of legislation. The Ordinance of 1787, more popularly known as the Northwest Ordinance, applied to the Old Northwest—the land north of the Ohio River and west

ply piles of dry leaves. Building a permanent cabin meant many days of hard work.

There was—at least at first—plenty of game available, and rivers and streams supplied a bountiful catch of fish. So except for the cold winter season, food was not a problem. Clearing and preparing land for planting was tough, though, especially if it was wooded. As a result, few farmers harvested much of a crop the first year.

Health hazards abounded on the frontier. Through both diseases and accidents, settlers had to "make do" with their own cures. Even after settlement had progressed well, doctors and midwives remained scarce. Frontier women frequently gave birth unassisted and all too soon arose to get on with the chores. Childhood mortality

The Ordinance of 1787, more popularly
known as the Northwest Ordinance,
applied to the Old Northwest—
the land north of the Ohio River
and west of Pennsylvania.

of Pennsylvania. The Ordinance allowed a territory to become a state, guaranteed freedom of religion and trial by jury, provided for public education, and outlawed slavery.

The Old Northwest soon attracted thousands of settlers from other areas, and they had better tools than earlier pioneers. Their axes and saws were sharper and more durable, and their rifles were more accurate. Otherwise, though, the life of a pioneer had not changed much over two centuries.

A pioneer family's first shelter was usually a lean-to consisting of two poles, a deerskin roof that slanted from the pole tops to the ground, and walls made from branches, dried grass, and mud. Their beds were sim-

was high. Considering the lack of sanitation and medical care, it is surprising that more of the pioneers didn't die at an early age.

Despite all the hardships, inconveniences, and dangers, for hundreds of thousands of people, the West spelled opportunity—a chance for a better life. The 1820 census counted 2.2 million whites living beyond the mountains, double the population of a decade earlier.

Native Americans Respond. The Indians had been given to understand that the Ohio River would be a permanent boundary between white

*Although founded by the French in 1701, Detroit was a key British outpost by the time of the Revolutionary War. This sketch shows how Detroit looked in 1780 when the British still had troops there.*

lands and their own. Based on a treaty the British had made in 1768, the only whites in the area at that time were fur traders and the residents of forts that the British had taken over after the French and Indian War. After the Revolutionary War, though, the Americans assumed that the British-Indian agreements were no longer valid. Besides, they believed the Indians should give up their land as punishment for having sided with the British during the Revolution.

On the surface, the Ordinance of 1787 appeared to be conciliatory toward the Indians. It promised that "Their lands and property shall never be taken from them without their consent; and in their property, rights and liberty they never shall be invaded or disturbed, unless in just and lawful wars authorized by Congress." Diplomacy was tried, but in the end it was war that decided the question of land ownership in the Ohio Country.

In the treaty ending the Revolutionary War the British had agreed to leave the Old Northwest, but British troops continued to occupy forts there. The British led the Indians to believe that the agreement making the Ohio River the white-Indian boundary still stood. They also continued

supplying the Indians with guns. Even without help, the Indians north of the Ohio were determined to resist white settlement. With British backing, they felt confident that they could turn back the tide of American settlement.

# War in Indiana.

President George Washington finally agreed that the federal government should finance and direct a war against the Indian tribes. In September 1790, General Josiah Harmar and his troops destroyed five deserted Miami towns near present-day Fort Wayne, Ind. Then they were ambushed and lost 40 militiamen and half as many regulars. A second skirmish between the troops and Indians left 133 whites dead and 31 wounded.

The U.S. Congress then authorized $300,000 for a second campaign which got underway on Oct. 4, 1791. Led by Arthur St. Clair, it was an even greater disaster than the first. Ambushed by a force of confederated tribesmen led by Miami chief Little Turtle, St. Clair's army suffered 630 killed and about half that number wounded.

The United States next tried negotiation. Secretary of War Henry Knox sent out three commissioners who were prepared either to cede back much of the land earlier acquired by treaty or to make the Indians a gift of $50,000 and an annuity of $10,000 for life if the treaties stood. Still confident of British support and their own eventual victory, the Indians refused both offers. They insisted on complete American evacuation of all land north of the Ohio. Since the Indians had no use for money, they ingeniously suggested that the Americans give the $50,000 and the $10,000 annuity to the Ohio settlers to help them move out.

**Fallen Timbers.** Washington decided to renew hostilities and called on Major General Anthony Wayne, a hero of the Revolutionary War whose reckless courage had earned him the nickname "Mad Anthony." With nearly $1 million and 6,000 troops at his disposal, Wayne planned carefully. He built forts along his line of march and sent out forward and flanking scouts to avoid an ambush. To counter Wayne, the Indians organized a force of about 2,000 Wyandot, Ottawa, Chippewa, Potawatomi, Miami, and Shawnee and, under a new commander, prepared to meet the Americans at Fallen Timbers, near present-day Toledo, Ohio. Although warned by Little Turtle to beware of Wayne, "a chief who never sleeps," the warriors were confident they could handle Mad Anthony just as they had Harmar and St. Clair.

Wayne delayed his attack until, after three days without food, great numbers of Indians went off to forage. At that point, on Aug. 20, 1794, Wayne struck. Although the loss of life on both sides amounted to fewer than 100, the Indians retired from battle. The following year, they agreed to the Treaty of Greenville. In exchange for $10,000 a year, they gave up the Ohio River boundary line. White settlements continued to replace Indian villages throughout what is now Ohio.

*In 1795, "Mad Anthony" Wayne dictated the terms of the Treaty of Greenville to the Indians. The inset portrait shows how Wayne looked in 1796, the year he died.*

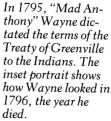

The Indians may have thought the Greenville boundary line, drawn in eastern Indiana, would last forever. The settlers harbored no such illusion. The right of the government to preempt land west of the line was written into the treaty and, with or without official action, white settlers intended to keep on moving west.

**T**ippecanoe. The next attempt by the Indians to win back the Old Northwest came in the early 1800's. In 1802 and 1809, William Henry Harrison, as governor of Indiana Territory, purchased huge tracts of land in what are now Indiana and Illinois. In about 1810, the Shawnee chief Tecumseh began to rally his people for another try at resistance.

Tecumseh traveled throughout the Old Northwest and the South in an effort to form a confederacy of Indian tribes that would eliminate the whites once and forever. He found many ready listeners, but it was far too late for the Indians to achieve such an objective.

While on his mission in the South, Tecumseh had left his one-eyed brother, known as the "Shawnee Prophet," in charge in Indiana. The Prophet's antiwhite agitation brought Harrison into action. Harrison organized a militia to march on the principal Shawnee town at the Wabash and Tippecanoe rivers, near present-day Battle Ground, Ind. There, in November 1811, the Indians launched a predawn attack, which Harrison's forces repulsed with heavy losses. The Prophet did not renew the fight and

*Not all encounters between settlers and Indians were unfriendly. This painting from 1820 shows a peaceful meeting along the Arkansas River between some Kiowa and other Indians and a group of explorers.*

*This color lithograph from the late 1880's is a highly fictionalized view of the Battle of Tippecanoe in 1811.*

the Shawnee withdrew, leaving Tippecanoe a victory for the whites.

Tippecanoe did not end Indian-white conflict on the Northwestern frontier, however. Within a year, it had merged with the larger British-United States conflict, the War of 1812. Tecumseh, along with many Shawnee, joined the British side. He fell in battle in Canada in 1813.

# The Black Hawk War.

The final resistance of Indians in the Old Northwest came in the early 1830's. Black Hawk, a Sauk chief, became the principal actor in the drama that unfolded along the Rock River in northwestern Illinois.

In 1804 at St. Louis, representatives of Sauk and Fox Indians agreed to cede land they occupied in southwestern Wisconsin and northwestern Illinois in exchange for trade goods valued at $2,234.50 and annuities totaling $1,000. However, one section of the treaty stated that Indians could live on and use the land "as long as the lands which are now ceded to the United States remain their property," and for more than 20 years nothing was done about removing them. Indians who opposed the treaty, like Black Hawk, would later cite that part of the treaty and their continued occupation as proof that their land along the Rock River had never been sold.

In the meantime, Black Hawk and Sauk warriors—known as his British Band—along with other Indians of the Old Northwest, supported the British in the War of 1812. After the war, the U.S. Army garrisoned Fort Crawford in southwestern Wisconsin, where the Wisconsin River flows into the Mississippi. Deposits of lead were discovered on Sauk and Fox lands, and in the 1820's miners moved into the area to exploit the mineral resources. Farmers soon followed the miners into the area.

With white settlement diminishing their game supply, the Indians became increasingly resentful of the intrusions. However, one Indian chief, Keokuk, considered the odds as being hopelessly in favor of the whites. So when he was informed in 1829 that it was time for the Sauk and Fox to move, he led a large number across the Mississippi into Iowa. Black Hawk, on the other hand, resisted. He did not agree to pull his British Band out of their ancestral homeland in the Rock River country until 1831.

Black Hawk had hopes of returning, however, and these hopes were reinforced when one of his lieutenants, Neopope, returned from Canada with the news that the British would help the Sauk and Fox get their land back. Neopope also reported that the Potawatomi, Chippewa, Winnebago, and Kickapoo would lend aid. As matters turned out, no British aid

Indians but brought more Sauk into combat. The militiamen lost 11 dead and several wounded as they fled pell mell from a battle known as Stillman's Run.

Sauk warriors, along with Potawatomi, now began raiding white farms. As additional militia arrived and federal troops joined in though, the odds against Black Hawk's success became overwhelming. He decided to move north into Wisconsin and from there, work his way back to safety in Iowa. As the Sauk moved, militia and regular army units pursued.

Game was scarce, and Black Hawk's people could take little time for hunting. The raids they made on

## Ignoring the Indians' attempts to surrender, white soldiers killed at least 150 men, women, and children, even wading out into the water to bayonet Indians as they fled.

materialized, and help from other Indian tribes proved minimal.

Rumors of a coming Indian uprising spread, and about 2,000 Indian men, women, and children returned to the Rock River country in the spring of 1832. The governor of Illinois called out the militia, which included 24-year-old Abraham Lincoln of New Salem.

Not long after returning, Black Hawk learned that he could not count on help from the Winnebago after all. He also learned that the Potawatomi would not supply food and that no British aid would be forthcoming. Discouraged, Black Hawk decided to surrender and sent three men out under a white flag. He also sent five observers. When the Illinois militiamen spotted the five observers—who were not under a white flag—they panicked and opened fire. They felled two

farms along the way did not produce enough food, and starvation soon began to thin their ranks.

At Wisconsin Heights on the Wisconsin River, a Sauk rearguard turned and fought while other Indians constructed makeshift boats and rafts to flee down the river to the Mississippi. Federal troops cut them off, however, killing most of them.

Leading another band, Black Hawk set off overland from Wisconsin but was trapped at a little stream called Bad Axe. Ignoring the Indians' attempts to surrender, white soldiers killed at least 150 men, women, and children, even wading out into the water to bayonet Indians as they fled.

Black Hawk got away. However, a band of Winnebago later turned him over to some soldiers. He was placed under a guard commanded by Lieutenant Jefferson Davis and impris-

In 1833, *Chief Black Hawk, right, and his son were taken East and displayed as prisoners of war.*

oned at Fortress Monroe until 1833. Black Hawk survived his imprisonment and later wrote his autobiography. He died in 1838.

# The Creek War.

Between the War of 1812 and the 1830's, the situation for Indians was the same in the South as in the Old Northwest. Native Americans fought and lost.

The Creek Indians of Alabama needed no reminders from Tecumseh to stir up their grievances against white encroachments on their lands. One group of Creek, called "Red Sticks," decided on action, and when the War of 1812 broke out, they began raiding white settlements.

In August 1813, the Creek, led by a half-breed Creek chief they called Red Eagle—who was known to whites as William Weatherford—attacked Fort Mims in Alabama and killed more than 400 whites who had fled there for safety. Willie Blount, governor of Tennessee, thereupon ordered militia commanded by Andrew Jackson to go to Alabama to avenge the massacre and subdue the Creeks.

Jackson first sent about 1,000 cavalry against a Creek village of about 200 on the Coosa River. The soldiers killed all the men in the village and took 80 women and children captive. Five soldiers were killed and 41 were wounded in the battle.

Next, Jackson himself moved on Red Eagle's group which had surrounded Talladega, a village of Creeks not participating in the war. There, on Nov. 9, 1813, Jackson's forces killed 300 Indians, losing only 15 men in the process. Red Eagle struck back in January, attacking Jack-

*Sequoya spent 12 years developing a written alphabet for the Cherokee language. His chief aim for this written language was to help preserve the tribe's ancient culture.*

son's encampment on the Talladega site, but the outcome was indecisive.

The Creek War's climax came at Horseshoe Bend on the Tallapoosa River in March 1814. Creek men, 900 strong, along with some 300 women and children, had dug in behind log fortifications to stake everything on a battle against 2,000 whites and a number of Cherokee under Jackson's command. After a day's fighting, the Creek had more than 750 dead. Jackson's losses amounted to 51 dead and 150 wounded. The Creek were later moved to lands west of the Mississippi.

# The Cherokee.

The Cherokee were unique among Native Americans: they successfully adopted the white way of life. Around 1800, the Cherokee began to shed their hunting and gathering ways and to rely exclusively on agriculture. They raised corn, cotton, and other crops; grazed livestock; and practiced crafts such as blanket weaving. Some Cherokee even owned black slaves.

One outstanding Cherokee — named Sequoya but often referred to by whites as George Guess — created a written form of the Cherokee language. The Cherokee printed books in their own tongue, and for six years they also published a newspaper, *The Phoenix.*

Cherokee hunters once roamed huge areas in Georgia and Tennessee. By 1820, however, land cessions had squeezed Cherokee holdings to a portion of northern Georgia, with smaller areas in southern Tennessee and northeastern Alabama. The desire of land-hungry Georgians for the remaining Cherokee lands brought the tribe considerable harassment throughout the 1820's from both individuals and the state government.

The Cherokee resisted, although not by armed force. Instead, they lobbied the federal government for favorable treatment. They even called on President Andrew Jackson to intercede. Jackson, however, upheld the idea of taking over Cherokee land and moving the Indians west of the Mississippi. As a last resort, the Cherokee turned to the Supreme Court of the United States, and the Court found that the Cherokee Nation constituted a separate political entity over which Georgia had no authority.

Although the decision seemed a triumph for the Cherokee, it proved to be a Pyrrhic victory because President Jackson refused to enforce it. Instead, he signed the Indian Removal Act of 1830. Plans to transplant the Cherokee to other lands proceeded.

Some Cherokee voluntarily left Georgia for the hills of Tennessee and North Carolina. The remaining 19,000 or so kept hoping for a miracle that did not materialize.

In the spring of 1838, some 10,000 white soldiers were assembled to herd the Cherokee west to Oklahoma. Most of the Indians had made no preparations and were forced to leave their possessions behind. At least 4,000 died along the way — of cholera, dysentery, fever, and in childbirth. The route they followed from Georgia to Oklahoma is now known as the Trail of Tears.

**The Seminole.** The Indian Removal Act of 1830 applied not only to the Cherokee but to the Seminole as well. Those Indians responded with force, just as they had on previous occasions when whites threatened to take over their ancestral lands.

In 1832, the Seminole War broke out when the Indians objected to being forced to leave Florida for Oklahoma. Chief Osceola and his Seminole warriors inflicted several defeats on the white troops. In 1837, however, Osceola was captured and imprisoned. Suffering from chronic malaria, he died in prison the following year. The Seminole War finally ended in 1842. In all, it cost the United States 1,500 lives and more than $20 million.

Some Seminoles agreed to give up their land and move west. Many resisted, though, and the government finally left them alone in their homeland in the Florida swamps.

**The Native American Dilemma.** In an 1829 letter to the Creek that urged them to accept removal, President Andrew Jackson wrote: "There your white brothers will not trouble you; they will have no claim to the land, and you can live upon it, you and all your children, as long as the grass grows or the water runs, in peace and plenty. It will be yours for ever." The Indians had heard those words before, and "for ever" meant until whites had a use for Indian land. Then, for Native Americans, the grass stopped growing and the water ceased to run. For white settlers such as the Davises and the Lincolns, though, things turned out quite differently.

*Prodded along the Trail of Tears by U.S. soldiers, the Cherokee took with them the few possessions they could carry. Many of the migrants left behind comfortable homes and rich farms. This version of the event was painted more than a century after it took place.*

In the early 1800's, many tiny communities sprang up in the wilderness as settlers found places where they wanted to start their new lives. Some of these villages prospered and grew.

eventually failed. Many of these tiny towns have completely disappeared. However, Lincoln's overall importance to history means that New Salem has been rebuilt and is now an Illinois

## NEW SALEM

Others, such as New Salem, Ill., Abraham Lincoln's home from 1831 to 1837,

State Historic Site. In 1831, a trader and store owner named Denton Offutt hired Lincoln,

then living near Decatur, Ill., as a boat hand for a trip down the Mississippi River. Impressed with young Lincoln's work on the boat, Offutt hired Abe to clerk in Offutt's New Salem store.

At that time, New Salem was a village of log cabins clustered around a grist mill, a barrel-maker's shop, and a few other stores and businesses. Lincoln's wages were low, and he slept in a room at the back of Offutt's business. Within a few months, though, the store failed, and Lincoln was out of a job.

Fortunately for Lincoln, the Black Hawk War soon started, and Lincoln volunteered for military duty. He served 90 days in the militia and didn't see any action, but he later recalled that he had many "bloody struggles with the musquetoes."

During his military service, Lincoln announced his candidacy for the Illinois state legislature. He arrived back in New Salem just two weeks before the election, which did not give him much of a chance to campaign. He lost the election, despite the

**Life on his own began for Abraham Lincoln when he settled in New Salem. At right is New Salem as it looks today.**

A restored shop in New Salem shows visitors today what kinds of items were available for purchase in Lincoln's time.

This restored cabin shows the way successful pioneers lived in the 1830's.

fact that 277 of the 300 voters in his precinct voted for him.

Having given up the militia and lost the election, Lincoln needed a job. He and a friend named William F. Berry decided to open up a general store in New Salem. However, like Offutt's store somewhat earlier, the new venture failed within a few months. Lincoln later said that the partnership with Berry "did nothing but get deeper and deeper in debt."

In May 1833, Lincoln became postmaster of New Salem. This job, along with a job as a deputy surveyor, earned him a living.

In 1834, Lincoln again ran for the legislature, and this time, he won. The same year, he started studying law. There were no law schools in those days, so potential lawyers simply read all the law books they could and then took the examination. Lincoln got his license to practice law on Sept. 9, 1836.

By that time, the population of New Salem had dwindled, and Lincoln decided to move to Springfield, Ill., the new state capital. He did not have much worldly wealth to show for his years in New Salem; all his belongings fit into his saddlebags. He arrived in Springfield on April 15, 1837. His years in New Salem were over.

Today, visitors to the restored New Salem village can see the Lincoln-Berry general store, Rutledge Tavern, the grist mill, and several other buildings. The exhibits also include several items that once belonged to "Honest Abe." Most of all though, the small settlement is a good example of living conditions on what was then the frontier of the new nation.

**Direkte till Amerika**

med

Anchor-Liniens Transatlantiska Ångbåts-Bolag

som betordrar Emigranter
med egna
för Emigrantbefordring afsedda
1:sta klassens ångare

**"Scandinavia" & "Scotia"**

från Göteborg hvarje Tisdag.

Tolkar medfölja från Göteborg ända till Chicago.

Göteborg år 1870.
**JOHN MILLAR,**
Anchor-Liniens Generel-Agent för Sverige.

GÖTEBORG.
Tryckt hos J. A. Brusberg

*Posters such as this
one from Sweden
appeared throughout
Europe to advertise
ships that were sail-
ing to America.
However, few of the
passengers could
probably afford
clothing such as this
reed bonnet, which
was considered
proper attire for a
young lady of the
mid-1800's.*

# CHAPTER 17: IMMIGRANTS AND THE NEW NATION

When Englishman Samuel Slater came to America, he carried more than the usual immigrant baggage with him. Along with a knowledge of the British textile industry, he had memorized the blueprints for a new, water-powered spinning machine. Slater had to rely on his memory because, to protect an important industry at home, British law prohibited the export of textile machinery, plans, or models. Aboard ship—according to legend—Slater passed himself off as a farmer, because law also prohibited the emigration of anyone who had knowledge of the design or operation of spinning machines.

In adopting the identity of a farmer, though, Samuel Slater did not tell an out-and-out lie. He had been born in 1768 into a farming family in Derbyshire. When he was 15, his father apprenticed him to one Jedediah Strutt, a stocking manufacturer. Near the end of Slater's apprenticeship, news reached Derbyshire that someone in Pennsylvania had won $500 for making a crude model of a spinning machine. Clearly, the Americans were very eager to develop manufacturing, and the events started him to thinking.

Slater's ambition had always reached beyond the life of a skilled worker. So after completing his apprenticeship, he stayed on with Strutt and became a supervisor. In addition to learning about management, he put in hours memorizing the mechanical details of various machines and kept his own counsel. Only at the last minute did he even tell his mother that he was emigrating.

Samuel Slater used the nearby Blackstone River to supply power for his first cotton mill.

Slater intended to go to Philadelphia but in New York he heard that Moses Brown, a thread manufacturer in Pawtucket, R.I., wanted to improve his company's operation. Slater wrote to Brown, offering his services "in making machinery, making good yarn, either for *stockings* or *twist*, as any that is made in England," and outlining his experiences in the Derbyshire textile mill.

Brown responded favorably, so Slater journeyed by stagecoach to Pawtucket. After viewing the factory, Slater pronounced Brown's machinery to be worthless. Brown hired him for $1 a day to direct the assembly of wood and iron parts into spinning machines equal to the best England had to offer.

In 1793, three years after Slater had his machinery in operation, a Yankee schoolteacher named Eli Whitney was visiting a Georgia plantation. While there, he invented the *cotton gin*, a machine that provided an easy way to remove the seeds from cotton, thus assuring New England mills of a domestic supply of that raw material. The swift-flowing streams of New England furnished power to run spinning and, later, weaving machines, while New England farm women—eventually replaced by immigrants from Italy and Ireland—supplied labor for the mills.

Samuel Slater's wages remained at a dollar a day for only a short time. He soon became a partner in the company and in 1792 realized about $1,500—nearly five times his previous wages—as his share of the profits. In 1798, Slater started his own company in Rehoboth, Mass., which soon was a great success. When he died in 1835, Slater was acclaimed throughout the nation for his achievements on behalf of American industry. His became one of the new nation's first immigrant-makes-good stories.

# Attitudes Toward Immigration.

The success of people such as Samuel Slater reflected the dream of America's future held by Alexander Hamilton, himself an immigrant from the West Indies. Hamilton—who was George Washington's first secretary of the treasury—envisioned America as a nation of cities and manufacturing in which immigrants would play a vital role as both workers and entrepreneurs. Accordingly, he believed the government should encourage and promote immigration.

On the other hand, George Washington and Thomas Jefferson had misgivings about unrestricted immigration. Washington was particularly dubious. In a letter to John Adams, he wrote:

> My opinion, with respect to emigration is that except of useful mechanics and some particular descriptions of men or professions, there is no need of encouragement,

while the policy or advantage of its taking place in a body (I mean the settling of them in a body) may be much questioned; for, by so doing, they retain the language, habits, and principles (good or bad) which they bring with them.

Jefferson was of two minds about immigration. His humanitarian side and his regard for liberty prompted him to welcome victims of oppressive governments to America. Yet his ideal America was a land in which small farmers would predominate, a nation whose population growth would depend more on natural increase than on immigration. Jefferson favored skilled artisans as immigrants, but not "the desolute and demoralized handicraftsmen of the old cities of Europe." He worried about the many immigrants who would come from nations ruled by absolute monarchies—characteristic of Europe at the time—and who would be unfamiliar with the liberty that prevailed in America. Jefferson suggested:

> They will bring with them the principles of the governments they leave, or if able to throw them off, it will be in exchange for an unbounded licentiousness, passing, as usual, from one extreme to the other. It would be a miracle were they to stop precisely at the point of temperate liberty. These principles, with their language, they will transmit to their children.

Hamilton's view of the United States of the future proved more accurate than Jefferson's. As for immigra-

---

## . . . George Washington and Thomas Jefferson had misgivings about unrestricted immigration.

---

tion, though the federal government did not actively promote it, few restrictions were placed on the influx of newcomers for nearly 100 years after the nation's founding.

Immigration and the Constitution. Delegates to the Constitutional Convention in Philadelphia in 1787 argued the immigration question on more than one occasion, particularly with respect to qualifications for holding public office. George Mason of Virginia upheld what became the majority view. According to James Madison:

> Col. Mason was for opening a wide door for emigrants; but did not chuse to let foreigners and adventurers make laws for us & govern us. Citizenship for three years was not enough for ensuring that local knowledge which ought to be possessed by the Representative.

In the end, delegates voted to fix residency requirements for members of the House at seven years and for members of the Senate at nine. As for the presidency, they decided that only an individual who was native-born could be the nation's chief executive.

The French Revolution. At first, Congress made the process of *naturalization*, the system by which foreigners could become citizens, relatively easy. The French Revolution changed that. Shocked by the short but violent Reign of Terror and France's combative stance in Europe, many Americans now backed away from their earlier enthusiasm for change in France.

A New Naturalization Act. The French Revolution produced two kinds of refugees, a number of whom came to the United States. One group consisted of royalists—people who had opposed revolution from the beginning. The royalists included thousands of whites who had fled the French colony of Haiti in the Caribbean after black slaves there revolted and took over the colony early in the 1790's. The other group was made up mainly of moderate revolutionaries who had fallen out of favor in France. In America, leaders of both the Federalists and the Democratic-Republicans viewed these immigrants as potential voters who might be relied on for support. The Federalists expected royalist support, while the Democratic-Republicans expected the support of the other refugees.

Members of the Federalist Party —the party of Washington, Adams, and Hamilton—treasured America's English heritage and found their most consistent support in New England. They were generally thought to be favorable toward business and commercial interests and the well-to-do. The Federalists welcomed opponents of the French Revolution and viewed anyone who even sympathized with such upheavals as a potential source of discord in America.

The Democratic-Republicans, led by Jefferson and Madison, were anti-British and pro-French. They were perceived as protectors of the interests of small farmers, artisans, and immigrant groups such as the Irish. The Democratic-Republicans welcomed those who sympathized with revolution.

However, when they considered recent French immigrants, both Democratic-Republicans and Federalists concluded that their parties would lose as much as they would gain should the newcomers become voters within two years. Accordingly, in 1795 Congress raised the residency requirement for citizenship from two years to five.

Naturalization in 1798. Naturalization came up again in 1798 with the passage of the Alien and Sedition

*One of the most famous—and wealthiest—immigrants of all time was John Jacob Astor. Born near Heidelberg, Germany, Astor came to America at age 20 and made a fortune in the fur trade. Eventually, his companies won an almost complete monopoly of the trade in the United States and had workers in far-flung, desolate environments such as the one shown here in Alfred Jacob Miller's "Setting Traps for Beaver."*

*Astor invested most of his profits in Manhattan Island farmland, which is today the heart of New York City. When Astor died in 1848, his fortune was estimated to be more than $20 million.*

American newspapers sometimes contained cartoons about the newest immigrants. This cartoon satirized both the world economic situation and the influx of poor Irish immigrants with the heading "The Balance of Trade with Great Britain Seems to Be Still Against Us."

Acts. Although initially passed to silence opposition to an expected war with France, the main focus now quickly became the Irish, not the French. Whether they marked Democratic-Republican ballots out of party loyalty or not, the Irish usually turned in a nearly solid anti-Federalist vote. They considered Federalists snobbish toadies of the British, whom the Irish hated.

In 1798, a failed rebellion in Ireland sent thousands of losers across the Atlantic to escape the gallows or long prison terms. The Federalists then decided it was time to strike a blow against participation by the "ignorant masses" in government and also time to deprive the Democratic-Republicans of votes. Senator Harrison Gray Otis of Massachusetts forthrightly explained the Federalist purpose:

> If some means are not adopted to prevent the indiscriminate admission of wild Irishmen and others to the right of suf-

frage, there will soon be an end to liberty and property. . . . I do not wish to invite hordes of wild Irishmen, nor the turbulent and disorderly of all parts of the world, to come here with a view to disturb our tranquility, after having succeeded in the overthrow of their own Governments.

Congress passed the Federalist-sponsored Naturalization Act of 1798, extending the waiting time for citizenship to 14 years. Presumably that would allow enough time to tame the "wildness" out of the Irish and other "undesirables," and make them fit candidates for citizenship. However, the law was not retroactive, which nullified any benefit it might have brought to the Federalists. In the election of 1800, naturalized Irish citizens, along with a great many Germans, voted overwhelmingly for the Democratic-Republican presidential candidate, Thomas Jefferson. The Federalists were turned out of power, and Republican-controlled Congress soon repealed the 1798 naturalization act, returning the waiting period to five years, where it remained.

**Curbing Criticism.** During the 1790's, political clubs and newspapers were founded to promote the Democratic-Republican point of view and offer strong and often abusive criticism of the Washington and Adams Administrations. Many immigrants still classified as *aliens*, or foreigners, belonged to the clubs. The Federalists had their own newspapers and groups to return the fire, but in 1798 they went further. Congress passed two acts dealing with aliens, including one that gave the President the power to deport all aliens:

> as he shall judge dangerous to the peace and safety of the United States, or shall have reasonable grounds to

suspect are concerned in any treasonable or secret machinations against the government thereof.

In addition, Congress passed the Sedition Act, which included a section making it a crime for anyone to criticize the President or Congress verbally or in writing.

The alien acts were never enforced, but the Federalists used the Sedition Act against several critics of the government. The first person arrested and jailed was Matthew Lyon, an Irish-American Republican congressman from Vermont, who was convicted for criticizing President Adams. However, by the time the Democratic-Republicans took over in 1801, the Sedition Act had become a dead issue, since it had been passed with a two-year limitation.

# Factors in Immigration. Even though the question of who were and who were not desirable candidates for

citizenship exercised Congress from time to time, newcomers from Europe hardly inundated the United States during the 40 years following 1775. The American Revolution, the French Revolution, the Napoleonic Wars, and the War of 1812 occupied western Europeans and curtailed transatlantic travel. After things quieted down, however, a huge wave of immigrants rolled westward across the sea.

*The Revolutionary War did not bring equal status to women in America. After the war, New Jersey briefly allowed women of property to vote, although this right was soon taken away. Some women fought for their rights, most notably Frances Wright, a Scottish immigrant.*

# THE LOUISIANA PURCHASE

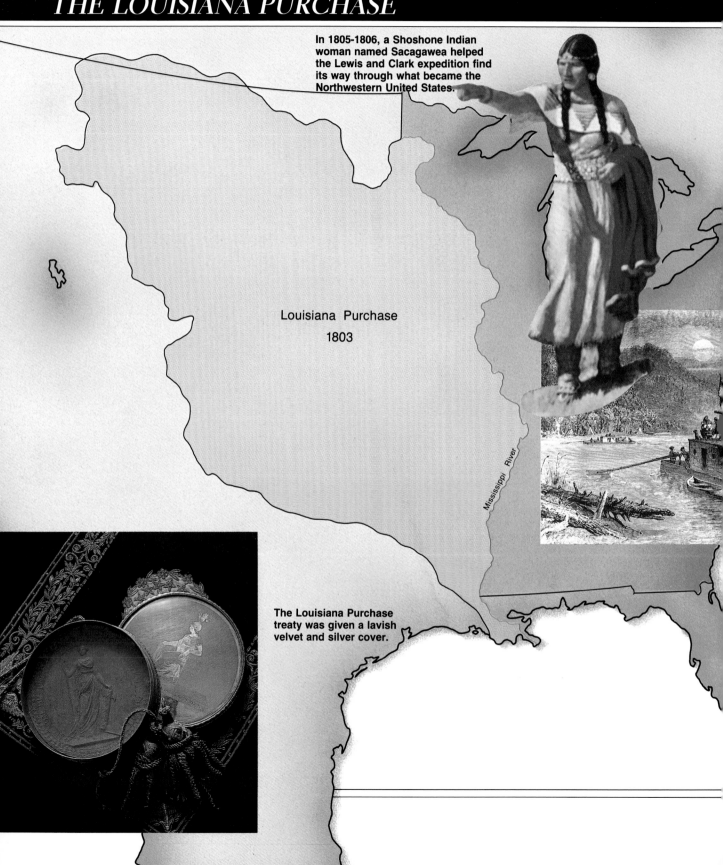

In 1805-1806, a Shoshone Indian woman named Sacagawea helped the Lewis and Clark expedition find its way through what became the Northwestern United States.

Louisiana  Purchase

1803

Mississippi River

The Louisiana Purchase treaty was given a lavish velvet and silver cover.

**Flatboats provided an easier and cheaper way to travel than did wagon trains.**

Many factors contributed to this surge in immigration between 1815 and 1860. One was a tremendous increase in the European population, resulting from better sanitation, the development of protection against diseases such as smallpox, and improvements in diet. Another factor was the development of large-scale farming and livestock production, which left thousands of farm families without land to work. In addition, the rapid growth of the factory system put large numbers of artisans out of work. The landless and the unemployed flocked to the cities, where they helped push up the cost of public welfare. Euro-

some, "elsewhere" meant another European country. To others, it meant South America or Canada. However, to about 5 million Europeans between 1815 and 1860, "elsewhere" meant the United States.

The major sources of immigration remained much as they had been during colonial times. Two million newcomers were Irish and Scotch-Irish. The German provinces contributed 1,500,000, and about 750,000 arrived from England, Wales, and Scotland. Switzerland, Norway, and Sweden contributed about 40,000 each. About 20,000 arrived from the Netherlands.

---

## European nations began to drop restrictions on emigration in order to reduce their own welfare costs and rid themselves of discontented people who might cause social unrest.

---

pean nations began to drop restrictions on emigration in order to reduce their own welfare costs and rid themselves of discontented people who might cause social unrest.

Political upheaval also contributed to emigration. Uprisings against the monarchies in Italy, Germany, and Austria-Hungary in the late 1840's failed, and many of the rebels sought other homes. Religious motives likewise played a role, with some Dutch, Norwegians, and Germans leaving home for greater freedom of worship. However, the number of religious refugees did not approach that arriving in America during colonial times.

Finally, letters from those who had left home, plus countless books and newspaper articles describing life and opportunities abroad, caused millions of Europeans to wonder if life elsewhere might not be better. To

**The Transatlantic Voyage.** The transatlantic traffic in timber, cotton, wheat, and other commodities from America to Europe increased greatly after 1815. On the return trip, many vessels became immigrant ships, and competition among them for passengers forced down the cost of passage.

Although the cost of transportation decreased, the hardships and hazards of the Atlantic voyage remained as great as they had been in the 1700's. Because the vessels were primarily cargo ships, life for immigrants below deck was still crowded and uncomfortable at best. At worst, passenger quarters became pestholes when cholera and dysentery struck. Food was poor, and the water supply frequently became tainted. The voyage still took from six weeks to two months—even longer in the face of

*Leaving their home in Europe was difficult for many immigrants, as shown here in the somber faces of a young couple leaving England in 1855.*

adverse winds and storms. Some ships struck icebergs and went down, some caught fire, and some developed leaks and sank—all at considerable loss of life.

# The Irish.
Conditions for the Irish in their homeland continued to be harsh. Farm rents were high, farm prices were low, and there was little opportunity for employment off the farm. About 260,000 Irish immigrated to America between 1820 and 1840.

Then disaster struck Ireland in 1845 with the appearance of the po-

tato blight. The failure of the potato crop deprived the Irish of a major food source and caused a devastating famine that lasted for several years. In 1847, a member of the Society of Friends reported from Ireland:

One poor woman whose cabin I had visited said, "There will be nothing for us but to lie down and die." I tried to give her hope of English aid, but, alas! her prophecy had been too true. Out of a population of 240 I found thirteen already dead from want. The survivors were like walking skeletons— the men gaunt and haggard, stamped with the livid mark of hunger—the children crying with pain—the women in some of the cabins too weak to stand. When there before I had seen cows at almost every cabin . . . but now all the cows were gone—all the sheep—all the poultry killed . . . the very dogs which had barked at me before had disappeared; no oats—no potatoes.

Between 1845 and 1851, Ireland's population declined by 2 million people. About 750,000 died of starvation and disease. The remainder emigrated.

The Irish immigrants, who had been largely a rural people, became city dwellers in America. In part, this was because they were so destitute when they landed that they could not afford transportation inland from their port of debarkation. Although some men became miners in the coal fields of eastern Pennsylvania, most left the cities only for temporary construction jobs on canals and railroads. Women often found employment in the textile and shoe factories or worked as domestic servants for wealthier Americans.

Between 1815 and the 1840's, many immigrants from Ireland were Scotch-Irish Presbyterians. The number of Irish Catholic immigrants increased rapidly, though, and they contributed much to the early growth of the Roman Catholic Church in America.

## Germans, Cornish, and Scots.

Few German immigrants settled in New England. Most arrived with enough money to travel to other parts of the country, and many journeyed on, particularly to the Ohio and Mississippi valleys. So many settled in Cincinnati, St. Louis, and Milwaukee that these cities became known as German towns.

*Ships not only brought poor immigrants to America, they also sometimes took those same immigrants back, as this cartoon shows. The luckier immigrants who found fortune in the "New World" sometimes made visits back to Europe to see family and old friends left behind.*

As they had in the 1700's, the Germans formed ethnic communities where they established some German-language schools and published their own books and newspapers. Many Roman Catholics as well as Protestants could be found among the Germans who immigrated to America after 1815.

Immigrants tended to gravitate to those areas where the jobs were plentiful and they could use whatever special skills they possessed. People who left Cornwall in southwestern England were an outstanding example of matching skill with opportunities for employment. In Cornwall, most men were miners, and in America, they of-

They were dominated by a middle class of government officials, clergy, professionals, and merchants. Although not persecuted, the peasants and artisans chafed at their lack of social equality, so many emigrated to America. Letters from those who found what they wanted kept the movement going.

"Here it is not asked what or who was your father, but the question is, what are you?" one said. "Farmers and artisans are just as good as merchants and officials," another immigrant wrote. Yet another said, "The clergy is not regarded, nor indeed regards itself, as better than the common people."

---

> # Immigrants tended to gravitate to those areas where the jobs were plentiful and they could use whatever special skills they possessed.

---

ten became lead miners in northwestern Illinois and southeastern Wisconsin. Some later left for jobs in the copper mines of Michigan's Upper Peninsula.

The Highlands of Scotland also experienced a potato blight in the 1840's, setting off a wave of immigration to America. In addition to farmers, many skilled weavers, tailors, shoemakers, and other artisans left Scotland for the "New World." For the most part, they took up their former occupations in America, where they settled in the East, South, and Middle West.

**S**candinavians and Dutch. In the 1800's, some 80 per cent of Norway's people were peasants and artisans.

During the 1840's and 1850's, thousands of Norwegians settled in south and central Wisconsin, northern Iowa, and southern Minnesota. Perhaps even more so than the Germans, the Norwegians transported and maintained their language, customs, and other cultural elements in the separate communities they often established.

Mass immigration from Sweden would come after the Civil War, but the seeds for a strong Swedish presence in America were sown earlier, in the 1800's. The Swedish population in the United States doubled in the century after 1750, reaching 3.5 million in 1850. A desire for land and jobs, plus economic hard times in Sweden in the 1840's, spurred the beginning of immigration. Swedish immigrants became farmers in the Middle West; lumberjacks in the pine forests of Michigan, Wisconsin, and Minnesota; and artisans and factory workers in Eastern cities.

Unlike most immigrants of the 1800's, many people came from the Netherlands in groups, as entire congregations of Protestants and Catholics arrived, led by pastors and priests. One group settled in southern Michigan in a community the immigrants named Holland. Another established the community of Pella in central Iowa. Still another created several communities in the Fox River Valley of Wisconsin.

Approximately 250,000 immigrants, scarcely 5 per cent of the total arriving between 1815 and 1860, settled in the South. Many newcomers who boarded ships bound for New Orleans merely transferred there to steamboats and journeyed up the Mississippi to the Middle West. Many immigrants saw few opportunities in the South, where factories were few and slave labor was abundant. In addition, many European immigrants did not care for the sultry, humid climate of the South which seemed so unlike the climate they had left at home. Overall, though, a great wave of emigration to the new nation had begun, and few, if any, factors would stem its flow from almost everywhere in the world for many decades to come.

*One immigrant who influenced many others to make the trip to America was Gustav Unonius. A Swede, Unonius wrote many letters about America that were published in Swedish newspapers and read by thousands. Although Unonius moved back to Sweden after 17 years in America, he continued to write fondly about his life in Wisconsin and Illinois in the 1840's and 1850's. His writings influenced many potential Swedish immigrants, such as the ones shown here.*

*Artist George Caleb Bingham was known for his paintings of ordinary people and frontier life. This painting, called* The Verdict of the People, *was completed in 1855.*

# CHAPTER 18: AN OUTBURST OF NATIVISM

In January 1836, there appeared in American bookstores a book entitled *Awful Disclosures of the Hôtel Dieu Nunnery of Montreal*. The author, Maria Monk, claimed to be a former resident of a convent called Hôtel Dieu. There had been books purporting to reveal the "secrets" of life in a convent before, and there would be more in the future. Maria Monk's, however, was among the few to make the best-seller list. Largely a tale of sex, sadism, debauchery, and violence, *Awful Disclosures* sold 300,000 copies over the next several years.

Inside the poster image:

**Fillmore & Donelson**
NATIONAL
**AMERICAN CLUB!**
**Muscatine, Iowa.**

We the undersigned, electors of the City of Muscatine and immediate vicinity, who are opposed to all sectional parties and in favor of the election of FILLMORE and DONELSON, respectfully invite the co-operation of all persons who are in favor of the principles of the National Fillmore American Party to assemble on

**SATURDAY EVENING**
THE 9TH, AT 8 O'CLOCK, IN FRONT OF THE
**AMERICAN HOTEL**

For the purpose of ratifying the Nominations of Fillmore & Donelson, and forming a National Fillmore American Club. John P. Cooke, Esq. State Elector, and Robt. McCartee, Esq. late of New York, will address the meeting.

An investigation revealed that Maria Monk had never been near Hôtel Dieu, let alone a resident of it. Her mother said Monk had suffered brain damage in a childhood accident and had spent some time in an asylum. However, Monk profited little from the book to which she affixed her name. In 1849, she was arrested on a pickpocket charge and died a short time later in jail. Who actually wrote *Awful Disclosures* is not known.

At any other time, the book probably would not have attracted overwhelming attention. In the 1830's, however, American feelings were running at full tilt against immigrants in general and Catholics in particular.

Cultural differences commonly arouse feelings of suspicion and even dislike between groups. Such feelings often produce stereotypes. *Nativism* goes further. It is a deep-seated antipathy by one group of people toward another. It is born of a fear that the second group intends to seriously damage, if not destroy, a way of life held dear by the first. Such feelings frequently generate hatred.

**C**ontributors to Nativism. In the 1790's, nativism, as well as a quest for votes, played a role in the controversies over naturalization. A more virulent *xenophobia*, or fear of foreign persons, was near its peak when *Awful Disclosures* appeared in bookstores. Numerous factors contributed to this outburst.

Many immigrants arriving in America after 1815 were poor, and this added to the number of people the extension of the right to vote to all males over age 21 regardless of whether they owned property. At the time, it was common for political party workers to meet immigrants at the ship on Election Day or the day before, take them before a judge who would grant naturalization for a few dollars a head, and then herd the new citizens to the polls to vote. The Democratic Party became particularly adept at the process. In addition, Democratic Party workers, among others, remembered immigrant families with baskets of food on holidays and with political favors whenever they were needed. Immigrants often tended to vote for Democratic candidates, not only because the Democrats wooed them, but also because

## Nativists deplored the tendency of many immigrants to cling to their Old World cultures.

seeking financial aid from the government in the crowded Eastern cities. By 1837, for example, about 60 per cent of the people in New York who received financial aid from the city were foreign-born. In Baltimore, Philadelphia, and Boston, more than half the occupants of almshouses were recent immigrants. Feeling already overburdened with taxes to care for native-born paupers, many prosperous Americans resented having to provide for people they considered outsiders as well. Many taxpayers also suspected—and there was some evidence to support the idea—that Great Britain and other countries were dumping their poor on America. In addition, many nativists seemed to believe much of the immigrants' poverty was due to intemperance and idleness.

Immigrants also were blamed for the political corruption that followed the Democratic Party presented itself—often very successfully—as the party of the common folks. Immigrants perceived the Whig Party much as they had the long-defunct Federalist Party—as the party of aristocracy and privilege.

The continued involvement of some immigrant groups in the politics of their homelands added to nativist complaints. For example, some Irish groups sent money and encouragement to organizations in Ireland that worked in various ways against Great Britain. Germans and Hungarians sometimes did the same for groups in their homelands in those nations.

Nativists deplored the tendency of many immigrants to cling to their Old World cultures. They also associated the Irish with the Roman Catholic Church and the church with practices of absolute control.

*Many political groups quickly learned that one way to get the immigrant vote was to help the newcomers locate jobs and to provide them with food.*

Catholics in America. The Roman Catholic Church is a hierarchical organization in which the members do not elect the leaders. Nor do the members of the church cast ballots of approval or disapproval on points of doctrine. In matters of faith and morals, Roman Catholics are expected to obey the church hierarchy above them. In the political realm, however, Catholics make their own choices. As Alexis deTocqueville put it in his famous book entitled *Democracy in America*:

American Catholic priests have divided the world of the mind into two parts; in one are revealed dogmas to which they submit without discussion; political truth finds its place in the other half, which they think God has left to man's free investigation. Thus American Catholics are both the most obedient of the faithful and the most independent citizens.

However, nativists refused to distinguish between the religious and the secular in their criticisms. Nativists pointed to the Vatican's condemnation of revolution and liberalism in Europe as proof that the Catholic Church was antidemocratic. If its highest leaders opposed democracy, how could its members uphold it? Judging Catholicism to be a grave danger to the nation, nativists followed in the footsteps of John Jay and others in the 1700's when they said that ridding America of this hated institution justified the use of almost any means.

## A War of Words.

One of the methods used by nativists posed no threat to life or limb. They launched a war of words on Catholicism through periodicals such as the *Reform Advocate*, the *Protestant Magazine*, and the *Native American*. Catholics responded by presenting their point of view in *The Truth Teller*, the *Metropolitan*, and the *Pilot*.

No plausible evidence of a Catholic plot to take over America was ever produced, despite the efforts of many nativist writers. For example, a famous Protestant minister named Lyman Beecher, in his *A Plea for the West* in 1835, "discovered" a conspiracy to take over the Mississippi Valley by inundating it with Catholic immigrants. About the same time, Samuel F. B. Morse, a painter, teacher of the deaf, and inventor of the Morse code, published *A Foreign Conspiracy Against the Liberties of the United States*, "exposing" the supposedly nefarious intentions of a Catholic missionary society.

During this era, nativist Protestant ministers often debated Catholic priests. The exchanges sometimes lasted for days, attracting large crowds but shedding more heat than light on the issues. Priests and ministers, of course, also presented their viewpoints in their Sunday sermons. However, Bishop John Hughes of New York did his cause little good when—in a sermon in St. Patrick's Cathedral—he proclaimed that a chief mission of the Roman Catholic Church was the conversion of all pagan and Protestant nations—"including the inhabitants of the United States."

## Violence.

Sadly, the war of words also sometimes erupted into violence. In 1829, after being aroused by a Protestant revivalist preacher, a mob attacked some Irish Catholic homes in Boston, continuing to stone them off and on for several days. Then in the early 1830's, some Irish immigrants in Charleston beat a native-born American to death. The following

*Presbyterian clergyman Lyman Beecher was noted for his fiery sermons on temperance as well as for his opposition to Roman Catholicism. Several of his 13 children also became well known, especially Harriet Beecher Stowe, who wrote* Uncle Tom's Cabin.

night, 500 nativists marched on the city's Irish section, tearing down and burning houses.

In 1848, Gaetano Bedini, a representative of the Vatican, toured America. Stirred up by the writings and speeches of a former priest, Alessandro Gavazzi, who condemned Bedini as a foe of democracy and liberty in Italy, a nativist mob in Pittsburgh roughed up the papal representative. In Baltimore, another mob burned him in effigy. In Cincinnati, a third mob, made up of German immigrants who blamed Bedini for helping to stifle democracy in their homeland, protested his visit. After parading through the streets with an effigy and gallows, they clashed with police and left 20 persons injured. At the end of Bedini's tour, a mob too large for police to handle awaited him at dockside in New York City. He had to be smuggled aboard his ship after it had left the harbor.

The worst rioting occurred in Philadelphia. It was caused by a controversy over the reading of the Protestant Bible in public schools. The school board had granted Bishop Francis Patrick Kenrick's request that Roman Catholic pupils be allowed to read their own version of the Bible and be excused from other religious activity. Tension began to build early in 1844 and led to rioting in May in the Irish-dominated suburb of Kensington, where one nativist was killed. Subsequent rioting led to 13 dead and at least 50 injured, as well as several burned-out city blocks. Investigating the turmoil, a grand jury blamed the Roman Catholics for trying to exclude the Bible from study in the public schools.

## Schools and Religion.

In the 1840's, American public schools were in effect auxiliaries of Protestant churches. Daily readings from the King James version of the Bible, prayers, and other religious activities

Complimentary Banquet to the Honorable Carl Schurz on the Seventieth Anniversary of his Birthday Thursday, March the second, 1899 Given by his friends at Delmonico's Fifth Avenue and Forty-fourth Street, New York

*Carl Schurz came to America after the failed European revolutions of 1848. He became a lawyer, campaigned for Lincoln in 1860, served as a Union general at the Battle of Gettysburg, was ambassador to Spain, and secretary of the interior. This menu is from an 1899 banquet in his honor.*

were common, and textbooks contained tales of pious morality. The Protestant slant in public education offended many Catholics. Their protests brought the nativist accusation that they were anti-public school, anti-Scripture, and un-American.

The school controversy grew warmer after the Provincial Council of Catholicity in America first met in Baltimore in 1829. The Council urged parishes to establish parochial schools for their children to avoid Protestant indoctrination.

Bishop Hughes waged a lengthy battle to wrest control of New York City's schools from the appointed— and also Protestant-oriented— Public

*This cartoon from the 1870's is typical of the concerns voiced by some people about the possibility of government funding for parochial schools.*

School Society and to obtain public funds for parochial schools. He succeeded in his goal of getting an elected school board, which gave Catholics some voice in selecting its members, but he failed to win support for public financing of Catholic education.

## Nativism and Politics.

In the 1840's, political parties were formed to further the native American cause. Although some won local offices and elected a few state legislators, these parties proved short-lived. In the 1850's, however, a new party espousing nativism enjoyed considerable success.

The new party grew out of a secret fraternal organization called the Order of the Star-Spangled Banner, founded in New York City in 1849. The order developed a ritual that included a promise not to vote for any

Catholic or foreign-born candidate and to work for the removal of Catholics and immigrants from public jobs. Membership grew rapidly, and members were notified about upcoming meetings by means of a heart-shaped piece of paper. For ordinary meetings, the paper heart was white, but if danger threatened, the paper heart was red.

In 1854, the organization's leaders transformed the group into the American Party. The American Party's name was well chosen. The slavery controversy had heated up, splitting the Whig Party and threatening trouble for the Democratic Party as well. The American Party provided these opposing factions with a common goal—the elimination of foreign influence on American institutions. One of the party's platform planks called for an extension of the waiting period for naturalization to 21 years. Another plank would deny public office to Roman Catholics and the foreign-born.

The American Party was commonly called the Know-Nothing Party, because each member of the original secret fraternity, when asked about the group, was instructed to say, "I don't know." If two members of the order were talking with nonmembers and one member began to speak too freely, the other would draw his thumb and forefinger across his eyes as a warning signal. Party members also used special handshakes and passwords.

The Know-Nothings did well in the 1854 elections. They captured control of state governments in Rhode Island, New Hampshire, Connecticut, and Maryland; elected local officials; and won seats in Congress. Before long, the country was flooded with products called Know-Nothing tea, toothpicks, and candy, while stagecoaches and even a clipper ship were also named *Know Nothing*.

The outlook for a national triumph and the presidency in 1856 seemed bright, and the American

Party nominated Millard Fillmore, who as Vice President had become President in 1850 upon the death of Zachary Taylor. As it turned out, Fillmore led the party not to victory but to oblivion.

In office, the Know-Nothings had not fulfilled the party's promise of action against Catholics and immigrants. Know-Nothings also shied away from a firm stand on slavery. To have taken a position against the extension of slavery would have cost the party Southern support. To have declared in favor of extension would have brought them trouble in the North, particularly in New England, where abolitionist sentiment was strong. By 1856, however, attitudes toward slavery in both North and South had hardened. Thus, Fillmore

received fewer than 75,000 votes, carrying only Maryland.

As it happened, Fillmore managed to carry Maryland only because of the "plug-uglies." These were gangs of toughs who stood in front of the polling places in Baltimore, armed with carpenters' *awls*—sharp tools for piercing holes—and threatened to "plug" anyone who did not know the party password and was not going to vote for their ticket. In some Baltimore wards, the plug-uglies carried guns to scare away Democratic voters. Other plug-uglies kept the Democratic turnout low by driving through the city's streets firing pistols.

With the election of 1856, anti-Catholic and antiforeign sentiment vanished from the foreground of American concerns. Instead, people focused their attention on a real danger to the nation—the breakup of the Union.

# PART 7: IMMIGRANTS AND WAR

After 1815, thousands of white settlers left the more settled Eastern regions of the continent for what were then the frontier areas, particularly Texas, the Great Salt Lake, and California. When the Civil War began in 1861, immigrant loyalties generally followed sectional lines. However, the war helped "Americanize" many immigrants, and it brought freedom to one group—African Americans.

*The Civil War brought destruction to cities such as Charleston, S.C., shown here, but the war also brought freedom to American blacks.*

*Pioneers traveling west on wagon trains and settling new territories sometimes faced robbers and other criminals, as well as hostile Indians. In Texas, settlers got protection from the Texas Rangers, who were organized in 1835.*

# CHAPTER 19: GOING WEST—TEXAS, UTAH, AND CALIFORNIA

Despite the successes of many in the new nation of the United States, not everyone prospered. Some saw the frontier as a solution to economic woes; others saw it as a religious haven. For these and a variety of other reasons, the movements westward continued—and increased—in the 1800's.

In 1819, a depression hit the nation. Banks failed, and businesses went under as the economy slowed. At age 54, Moses Austin, a successful lead mine operator in Virginia and Missouri, found himself to be one of those left broken by hard times. Austin decided to pursue an idea that involved unknown

*There were few trees on the Great Plains, so settlers often built their homes out of sod bricks, as shown here. The thousands of men who headed to California in search of gold also faced stark conditions.*

territory. In 1820, he set out alone from Missouri to ride 800 miles (1,287 kilometers) to San Antonio de Bexar, the seat of government for the province of Texas in the Spanish colony of Mexico. There, Austin called on the provincial governor, Antonio de Martínez.

Learning that his visitor was an American, Martínez informed Austin that if he were still in town at dawn the next day, he would be arrested. The Spanish had had their fill of *norteamericanos* and their political ideology of revolution.

The American and French Revolutions had been followed by movements for independence throughout the Spanish colonies and in Brazil, which belonged to Portugal. In Mexico, a revolution for independence had begun in 1810. It was led by two priests, Miguel Hidalgo y Costilla, known as "The Father of Mexican Independence," and José María Morelos y Pavón, who organized armies made up mostly of peasants. However, Spanish forces defeated the rebels, captured the two priests, and eventually executed each of them.

*Stephen F. Austin favored United States annexation of Texas, but he died before the task was accomplished.*

Americans had applauded the independence movements in Latin America. Some had even volunteered to help the Mexicans achieve freedom, joining expeditions into Texas to fight the Spaniards. However, some of these volunteers aimed to detach Texas politically from Mexico and establish an independent republic. The dust had hardly settled on the latest effort to do that—led by a Dr. James Long—when Moses Austin arrived in San Antonio.

A **Plan for Colonization.** The Spanish response to these expeditions and their participants was harsh. After defeating the invaders, Spanish authorities executed or drove from Texas every American they could find. By 1820, that vast region was inhabited by about 30,000 Indians and fewer than 4,000 whites.

From the white point of view, Texas needed people, and that is what Moses Austin planned to provide.

However, Governor Martínez' order prevented Austin from even mentioning his proposal. Glumly, Austin left the governor's office to prepare for the long journey back to Missouri. At that point, he happened to run into an old friend he had known in Louisiana—Felipe Enrique Neri, called the Baron de Bastrop—who had influence with the governor.

Neri arranged for Austin to meet with Martínez again, and together they persuaded the governor that American colonization would benefit Spain. The Spanish were sold on two ideas. One was that colonists would be a buffer against the Indians. The second was that the immigrants, being landowners and slaveholders, would not be revolutionaries but rather law-abiding citizens with a stake in discouraging change. The governor recommended Austin's plan to higher authorities, and they agreed.

In January 1821, with a grant of Texas land and permission to settle 300 immigrant families on it, Moses Austin began his return journey to Missouri. The journey home was even rougher than the outbound trip had been, and by the time he reached his destination he was exhausted. Soon after arriving home, Austin died, never to see his colonization plan reach fruition. However, his son, Stephen, aged 28, knew the plan well. A college graduate who had served in the Missouri territorial legislature, Stephen Austin was becoming as astute a businessman as his father had been. Along with his father's Texas land grant, Stephen Austin got the task of carrying out the region's colonization.

T **he First Immigrants.** By this time, Mexico had achieved independence from Spain. Texas became a Mexican—rather than a Spanish—province, and the colonial capital of Mexico City became the seat of government.

Given a choice of land, Stephen Austin selected a region between the Colorado and Brazos rivers. It was an area of fertile soil, well-watered and timbered. Each farming family would be entitled to 177 acres (72 hectares), while those planning to establish ranches were allowed 4,428 acres (1,792 hectares). To get the maximum amount of land, many immigrants who actually planned to grow cotton said they intended to raise cattle. Land was initially priced at 12¼ cents per acre (0.4 hectare), but many settlers got it for less.

Austin had no trouble finding candidates for immigration, for word of mouth had preceded the advertisements he placed in newspapers. Most of the new immigrants came from Louisiana, Alabama, Arkansas, and Missouri. At the time, the United States government was selling land for $1.25 per acre—and much of it was not nearly as fertile as the land that Austin controlled. Austin screened the applicants carefully, weeding out frontiersmen whose main occupation was hunting, as well as known drunkards, gamblers, "profane swearers," and those with reputations as idlers.

Once the agreed-upon 300 families had been settled in Texas, Austin applied for, and received, additional land grants. By 1835, he had increased the population of Texas by 1,500 families.

Austin had the power to name his own local government officials. His settlers were exempt from paying taxes for six years and also from paying tithes to the Roman Catholic Church of Mexico. The immigrants' main obligation, as far as Mexican authorities were concerned, was to defend the northern part of the nation.

Individuals besides Austin also received land grants and permission to bring immigrants to Texas, and by 1830, the American population there amounted to about 20,000. That was five times the number of Spanish-speaking inhabitants.

**C**ultural Differences. During those early years, officials in Mexico City paid little attention to the Texas settlements 1,200 miles (1,930 kilometers) to the north. There was practically no Texan trade with Mexico,

*Cowboys got their start in Texas. Many Mexican cowboys remained in Texas after it declared its independence from Mexico in 1836.*

but considerable traffic developed with the United States. Texans shipped out an estimated $500,000 worth of cotton, beef, hides, and mules in 1832, with cotton leading the list in value.

By then, Mexican officials had taken steps to exert tighter government control over their far northern province. However, cultural differences—and, more importantly, the imperialistic desires of the Texans—would make closer relations extremely difficult.

Language was a major obstacle. The Mexicans spoke Spanish, the Texans used English, and few people spoke both. Nor were there many opportunities to learn each other's language, since the two groups tended to live and work apart.

One area in which the Texans did not want to be regulated was slavery. In 1829, the Mexican government outlawed slavery. Most white immigrants from the United States, however, had come from slave states and saw no reason to abolish the institution, especially since the province's cotton and sugar cane fields depended on some 1,500 black slaves—unwilling immigrants—for labor.

Such attitudes dimmed the chances for peaceful coexistence. Reconciliation of differences would be difficult, if not impossible.

**Fear of Takeover.** Reflecting on the rapid territorial expansion of the United States after the American Rev-

## When the United States obtained Florida in 1819, it renounced all claims to Texas forever.

Religion was another divisive issue. Almost all Mexicans were Roman Catholic. Even those who seldom went to church believed firmly in baptism, marriage, and burial in the Roman Catholic Church, and they honored the various religious festivals that had become traditionally Mexican. The great majority of Texas settlers, on the other hand, were Protestant even if they seldom went to church, and they had all the anti-Catholic prejudices held by many Protestant people at that time.

The Mexican government expected loyalty to the nation and compliance with its laws. Texans were willing to be loyal—provided they were left alone and had as little regulation as possible from the Mexican government and its officials.

olution—with the Louisiana Purchase in 1803 and the acquisition of Florida 16 years later—Mexican officials saw clearly that the growth of the United States had been accomplished at the expense of Spanish-speaking people. Furthermore, the Mexican leaders had reason to believe—and fear—that the United States planned further expansion. When the United States obtained Florida in 1819, it renounced all claims to Texas forever. Still, in the 1820's there was talk about buying the part of Texas lying north of the Sabine River, and President John Quincy Adams expressed his willingness to pay $1 million for the land.

As far as Mexicans were concerned, however, not an acre of their nation was for sale. Many Mexican

# LAND ACQUISITIONS IN THE WEST

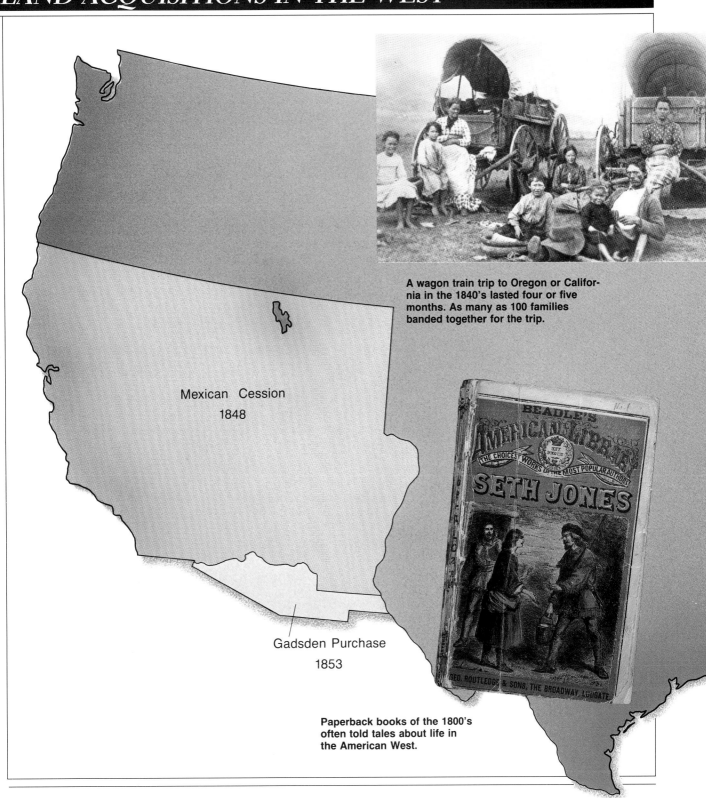

A wagon train trip to Oregon or California in the 1840's lasted four or five months. As many as 100 families banded together for the trip.

Mexican Cession
1848

Gadsden Purchase
1853

Paperback books of the 1800's often told tales about life in the American West.

*When Texas received statehood in 1845, the flag that had been used for the Republic of Texas became the new state's flag.*

government officials concluded that the whole Austin immigration effort had been just the opening move in a larger U.S. plan to take over a lot of Mexican land.

Accordingly, in 1830, the Mexican government applied custom duties to goods brought into Texas from the United States and, at the same time, prohibited further immigration. However, the Mexican government did not have enough troops to enforce its orders — so both trade and immigration continued.

# Movement toward Separation.

Although the Mexican government's changes did not please most Texas settlers, the majority saw no reason to rebel or go to war over them. Instead, the settlers organized a convention to draw up resolutions presenting their grievances. One of the resolutions requested a renewal of immigration. Another asked for Texas statehood within the Mexican union and included a state constitution. In April 1833, Stephen Austin set off for Mexico City to present the resolutions to government officials.

The government agreed to reopen immigration. Later, the government of the state of Coahuila—of which Texas was now a part—passed laws that favored the Texas settlers. One law allowed them to have three representatives in the state legislature of Coahuila, another law permitted the use of the English language for official business, and a third law granted them the right to trial by jury.

However, Mexican officials refused to grant Texas statehood. The Mexican constitution required that a territory seeking to become a state have 80,000 residents, and Texas fell far short of that. Besides, government officials considered the state constitution presented by Austin actually to be a deliberate step toward separation from Mexico, and it appears that some Texas leaders were thinking just that. One of these leaders was Virginia-born lawyer Sam Houston, a former congressman and governor of Tennessee, and a recent Texas arrival who had helped write the proposed constitution.

In January 1834, on his way back to Texas, Stephen Austin was arrested, accused of continuing to advocate statehood, and charged with treason. He was returned to Mexico City, where he was detained for 18 months, part of the time in prison.

In July 1835, Austin was allowed to leave Mexico City. By this time, he was firmly committed to Texan independence. In a letter to a cousin, he spoke of his hope for massive immigration to Texas to help achieve that goal:

> . . . A great immigration from Kentucky, Tennessee, etc., *each man with his rifle* . . . would be of great use to us—very great indeed. . . . For fourteen years I have had a hard time of it, but nothing shall daunt my courage or abate my exertions to complete the main object of my labors to *Americanize* Texas. This fall and winter will fix our fate—a great immigration will settle the question.

**F**rom Independence to Statehood. By the autumn of 1835, the majority of Texans had also swung toward separation. They organized a temporary government, and Texas troops, led by Colonel Benjamin Milam, attacked San Antonio. On December 11, the Mexicans surrendered.

The fall of San Antonio alarmed General Antonio López de Santa Anna, who had become the ruler of Mexico. On Feb. 23, 1836, Santa Anna launched a successful counterattack against the 187 Texans who had taken their stand in the Alamo, a mission outside the town. Almost all the people in the Alamo were killed, but the event is held in great reverence by Texans today, despite the failure.

Two more battles swiftly ensued—Goliad, in which the Mexicans were once again victorious, and San Jacinto, in which the tables were turned and Texan troops commanded by Sam Houston defeated the Mexicans. Although Santa Anna fled the battlefield, he was later captured. As president of Mexico, he recognized Texan independence, and Houston paroled him.

Texas now became a nation, and Sam Houston won election as president of the Lone Star Republic. Immigrants from the United States and abroad continued to add to the new nation's population. For example, thousands arrived from Germany to establish east Texas communities such as New Braunfels and Fredericksburg. Many Germans were outspokenly against slavery, which did not help relations with their neighbors. Even so, German farmers enjoyed a reputation for industriousness, thrift, and dependability.

Most Texans wanted statehood, but efforts to bring it about were complicated by the issue of extending slavery. Finally, in the closing days of President John Tyler's Administration, Congress annexed Texas by joint resolution. It became the 28th state in December 1845.

*By 1840, the Republic of Texas had a capital—Austin—with a grand house on a hill for the country's president. There was also an official seal for important documents.*

*During the Mexican-American War, U.S. General John E. Wool and his staff posed for this 1846 daguerreotype,* an early kind of photograph, *in Saltillo, Mexico.*

**The Mexican-American War.** Upon the admission of Texas, Mexico and the United States became involved in a dispute over the new state's southern boundary. The United States insisted on the Rio Grande, while Mexico claimed the boundary to be the Nueces River, farther north. President James K. Polk ordered American troops into the disputed area, where they built a fort blockading the Rio Grande. A month later, Mexican soldiers fired on a detachment of Americans, killing or wounding 16. In May 1846, Congress declared war on Mexico.

During the course of the war, the American soldiers sometimes changed sides and fought against their former comrades. The decades of the 1830's and 1840's were a time of considerable anti-Catholic and anti-Irish activity by nativist groups in the United States. The hostility made some Irish soldiers in the U.S. Army receptive to Mexican appeals that Catholics should band together:

> Can you fight by the side of those who put fire to your temples in Boston and Philadelphia? Come over to us! May Mexicans and Irishmen, united by the sacred ties of religion and benevolence, form only one people.

The Mexican leaders promised that U.S. deserters would receive Mexican citizenship and free land.

One of the first Americans to desert was Sgt. John Riley of the Fifth U.S. Infantry. He was followed by about 200 more deserters, who formed the nucleus of the San Patricio Company, or Company of St. Patrick. (The rest of the unit was made up of foreigners living in Mexico.) The unit carried a green flag showing a shamrock, harp, and St. Patrick.

The San Patricios fought fiercely at the battles of Buena Vista and Churubusco. The latter ended with a defeat for the Mexican Army. Riley was captured and sentenced to hang. However, United States General Winfield Scott reduced the sentence to 50 lashes with a rawhide whip, branding of the letter D (for deserter) on the cheekbone, and a dishonorable discharge. Scott's explanation for his action was that Riley had deserted before the United States officially declared war and therefore did not deserve to be executed.

Riley later rejoined his Mexican unit, rising to the rank of colonel. In 1849, he returned to the United States, where he sued the government for $50,000 for its treatment of him. He lost the case.

The Mexican-American War ended in 1848. The Treaty of Guadalupe Hidalgo, signed that year, gave the United States what are now the states of California, Utah, and Nevada, and parts of Wyoming, Colorado, Arizona, and New Mexico. This was about one-third of Mexico's territory. For its part of the exchange, Mexico received $15 million from the United States. Later, under the Gadsden Purchase of 1853, Mexico ceded land that extended the boundaries of Arizona and New Mexico south of the Gila River, and it received $10 million in exchange.

With Texas a state and with the addition of new territory after the Mexican-American War, the United States acquired a Spanish-speaking minority. For the most part, Mexican Americans were treated like second-class citizens. They lived in segregated housing and were employed almost exclusively as farm laborers.

*Traveling by wagon train was hard and dangerous, and not everyone survived the trip, as shown in this 1850 painting called* Prairie Burial.

*Joseph Smith was just 25 years old when he and five associates founded the Church of Jesus Christ of Latter-day Saints at Fayette, N.Y., on April 6, 1830.*

# A New Religion.

The decade or so following the War of 1812 had witnessed an outburst of enthusiasm for religion in America known as the second Great Awakening. (The first Great Awakening had occurred in the 1730's.) Revival meetings were held everywhere. New sects formed as offshoots of the Methodist, Presbyterian, and Baptist churches. Reports of religious visions were a common occurrence. One who said he had such visions was Joseph Smith, Jr., a young man in New York, who founded the Church of Jesus Christ of Latter-day Saints—otherwise known as the Mormon church. The group's religious teachings were set down in the Book of Mormon, which was first published in 1830.

In Ohio and Beyond. As word went out, converts flocked to the new religion, and in 1831, Smith established a community in Kirtland, Ohio, for the Saints, which is what Mormons called themselves, just as the earlier Puritans had called themselves. At first all went well, as the Saints bought land and started a bank. They soon fell into difficulty, though, due to the high prices of goods and their inability to pay. At the same time, opposition to the Mormons grew among the Gentiles, which is what the Saints called people who were not Mormons.

power and economic might. The likelihood of bloc voting in county and state elections worried many non-Mormons, who were also concerned by the Mormons' formation of their own militia, the Nauvoo Legion. The Mormon emphasis on cooperative living and the close association between church and state in Nauvoo was also worrisome to many of the non-Mormons.

Then, in 1843, following a revelation, Joseph Smith declared *polygamy*—plural marriage—to be a part of the Mormon way of life. Men could take more than one wife, although women were limited to one husband. Smith based his proclama-

---

## As the number of Mormons in Nauvoo grew, so did their political power and economic might.

---

The history of the Mormons over the next several years was one of a constant growth in numbers, accompanied by periodic dissension within the ranks and problems with Gentile neighbors. In 1838, the Mormons left Kirtland for a community in Missouri. Soon driven out, they went to Nauvoo, Illinois, on the east bank of the Mississippi. Nauvoo seemed like an ideal place, but it was not to be the final Zion—God's city on earth—that the Mormons sought to establish.

Prosperity in Nauvoo. The Mormons prospered in Illinois, and Nauvoo's population soon grew to 20,000 or more. Many converts came from England, Germany, Switzerland, and Scandinavia to join the Saints.

As the number of Mormons in Nauvoo grew, so did their political

tion on Biblical references to concubinage among the ancient Israelites during the time of Abraham. However, the Biblical references notwithstanding, polygamy scandalized most Americans. It also created a deep rift in the ranks of the Saints themselves.

Disaster and Movement West. Shortly after Smith proclaimed polygamy, a splinter group of Mormons began an opposition newspaper. Its first issue charged Smith with immorality. As a result, the first issue also proved to be the last. The paper was destroyed, and Smith was blamed for the destruction.

Smith and his elder brother Hyrum were arrested and jailed in the nearby town of Carthage. On June 27, a mob stormed the lockup, seized the prisoners, and lynched them. The

*Beginning in 1850, Mormon missionaries were sent to Europe to tell families, such as the one above, about a new Zion. By the end of the century, more than 12,000 Mormons had emigrated from Denmark alone to the United States.*

exodus of the Saints from Illinois and the destruction of Nauvoo soon followed.

Brigham Young, who became the new Mormon leader, and other prominent Saints agreed that the only solution to their troubles lay in emigration from the United States. After much study and discussion, they selected the valley of the Great Salt Lake in present-day Utah as their destination. There, in Spanish territory where no white settlements existed, the Mormons might be free from opposition to their religion.

The Saints gathered at Council Bluffs, Iowa. Then, in the spring of 1847, an advance party of 143 men, 3 women, and 2 children, led by Brigham Young, set out on the 1,000-mile (1,600-kilometer) journey across the Great Plains and the Rocky Mountains. They pioneered the Mormon Trail, along the north side of the Platte River through Nebraska and into Wyoming, across the river at Fort Laramie, then southwest to the Great Salt Lake. Finally they reached their

destination, and they were pleased. Said one member of the vanguard party:

I could not help shouting "hurra, hurra, hurra, there's my home at last." . . . The sky is very clear, the air delightful and all together looks glorious, the only drawback appearing to be the absence of timber. But there is an ocean of stone in the mountains to build stone houses and walls for fencing. If we can only find a bed of coal we can do well and be hidden up in the mountains unto the Lord.

The Mormons had found Zion at last. Thousands of immigrants soon followed. A year later, they learned that the Treaty of Guadalupe Hidalgo had put them back where they had

started—in the United States. Nevertheless, at least temporarily, the Mormons had achieved the isolation they sought. In 1860, Utah had a population of 9,000—and only 300 of them were non-Mormons.

With irrigation and hard work, the Mormons made the desert bloom. Mormon missionaries continued to be active, and thousands of converts from the United States and European countries crossed the plains to join the Mormons in the valley stretching north and south from the Great Salt Lake.

One result of the irrigation farming the Mormons practiced was the development of certain principles of water use that have since become part of the water law of all the Western states. One principle was that using water for irrigation was a "natural"

use—like drinking, cooking, and washing—rather than an artificial use—like milling, manufacturing, or mining. People who used water for natural reasons did not need a special permit from the state legislature. Nor did they have to return the water they used to the stream.

A second principle was known as the "right of prior appropriation." It stipulated that if an individual settled on the lower part of a stream, a later arrival who settled higher up the stream could not use so much of the water that not enough would be left for the earlier settler.

For many years, the polygamy issue blocked the territory's path to statehood. However, after the Mormons abolished plural marriage, Utah joined the Union in 1896 as the 45th state.

*In 1847, the Mormons first set out from Iowa for the Great Salt Lake. Fifty years later, the survivors of those 1847 trips gathered for this photograph, taken at the 1897 Utah Pioneer Jubilee. The celebration also included a parade and fireworks.*

*Although thousands of immigrants hoped to get rich in California by panning for gold, others, such as Bavarian immigrant Levi Strauss, shown below, acquired wealth in other ways. In 1874, Strauss began making riveted blue denim jeans and jackets. Today, Levi Strauss & Co. is the world's largest clothing manufacturer.*

The Quest for Gold. In January 1848, gold was discovered along the American River at Sutter's Mill, near what is now Sacramento, Calif. News of the discovery of gold spread rapidly, and by June, half of San Francisco had left town to seek the riches in the Sacramento Valley. San Jose was practically deserted, and towns as far south as Los Angeles lost sizable percentages of their people to the gold fields. News of the gold strike spread south—to the nations of Mexico, Chile, and Peru—and across the Pacific Ocean—to Australia and China. Thousands of people, about 95 per cent of them men, set out to seek their fortunes in the mountains of California. Between early 1848 and the end of 1849, these so-called "Forty-Niners" increased California's population from about 15,000 to more than 100,000.

At first, prices soared in California for everyday necessities. By 1849, flour sold for $44 a barrel, potatoes were $16 a bushel, and eggs cost $10 a dozen. This terrible inflation of prices led to an influx of goods from all over the world.

The Chinese and Others. Between 1848 and 1854, several hundred thousand people from all over the world poured into California. Despite this mingling, some groups were more tolerated by their fellow miners than were others. Among those most persecuted were those immigrants from France, Mexico, Chile, and China. The French were looked upon as clannish and were snubbed by others for that reason. The miners from Latin America, especially Mexico and Chile, were specially taxed and so badly treated that they eventually quit prospecting for gold. The Chinese were the miners who were most violently discriminated against. They were allowed to mine only in the worked-over sites that white miners had abandoned, and they had to pay a special tax which generated about half the state income from 1850 to 1870.

*The distinctive dress of Chinese gold miners was often ridiculed. Most Chinese men continued to wear the loose blouses, baggy pants, and cloth slippers that were the traditional apparel in their homeland.*

*Few of the Chinese immigrants were women. By 1890, the ratio of male to female ran as high as 27 to 1.*

In March 1865, Charlie Crocker began hiring Chinese workers to help build his Central Pacific Railroad. The work was hard, there was a shortage of white labor, and hiring the Chinese was something of a last resort. However, the Chinese were industrious, uncomplaining, and worked for lower wages—about $30 a month, paid in gold—than white laborers did.

By May 10, 1869, when the Central Pacific met the Union Pacific in Promontory, Utah, 90 per cent of the Central Pacific workers were Chinese. However, at the festivities at Promontory and elsewhere, the Chinese were excluded.

In the thriving economy of California and the West, the Chinese then found work as field hands, household servants, fishers, and construction workers. Some were able to start their own businesses, especially restaurants and laundries. However, an economic depression in the mid-1870's led to terrible incidents of violence against the Chinese, who were looked upon as taking scarce work away from other "real" Americans. In 1871, a mob in Los Angeles lynched several Chinese workers. Eight whites were convicted, but all were out of jail in less than a year. In 1885, an argument over who should dig in which coal vein caused a white mob in Rock Springs, Wyo., to kill 28 Chinese and wound 15 others. Sixteen whites were arrested but then released when a grand jury found that "no one was able to testify to a single criminal act by a white person that day." The cities of Seattle, Denver, and Tacoma also had anti-Chinese riots.

Few battles in American history have stirred the imagination and aroused so much emotion as the brief and bloody engagement between a handful of Texas settlers and a Mexican Army of thousands. The major battle took place on March 6, 1836, at an old mission called the Alamo on the outskirts of San Antonio.

In December 1835, a small band of rebellious Texas settlers had forced the surrender of Mexican troops in San Antonio and taken over the Alamo. Enraged, Mexican leader Santa Anna marched north with an army to retake the occupied mission and put down the rebellion before it went further.

On Feb. 23, 1836, Santa Anna's army surrounded the Alamo and began an 11-day siege with several thousand well-trained Mexican troops. The Alamo's defenders never numbered more than 200.

Moreover, the defenders were an assemblage of individualists rather than a disciplined fighting force. William Travis, at only age 26, eventually became commander. Travis had come to Texas in the early 1830's. Sent to the Alamo on February 3, Travis had expected to assume command, only to be disappointed and angered when the defenders chose James Bowie instead.

James Bowie, better known as Jim, at age 40, was a San Antonio resident with extensive landholdings and had early cast his lot with the rebels. He suffered from tuberculosis, however, and he turned command over to Travis after a fall that broke several ribs confined him to bed.

# THE ALAMO

**Jim Bowie fought with the small force at the Alamo.**

After the Battle of the Alamo, right, Santa Anna, above, was elected president of Mexico in 1833, but he did not serve. In 1834, he took control of the country, and he ruled as a dictator.

Perhaps more famous than either Travis or Bowie was former Tennessee Congressman David Crockett, known as Davy. Nearly 50 years old and recently defeated for reelection to the House, he had come to Texas with a small group of land-hungry adventurers. Crockett was the archetypal frontiersman—brave and a crack shot but also boastful and a teller of tall tales. He was already a legendary figure, and his death at the Alamo only heightened his mythic stature.

At dawn on March 6, Santa Anna's army ended the siege and squadrons

**Sam Houston won his greatest victory in the Battle of San Jacinto.**

**Today, the Alamo is one of the most popular tourist attractions in America's Southwest.**

**Davy Crockett had a colorful life and heroic death.**

carrying assault ladders and weapons dashed forward to scale the walls. Hopelessly outnumbered, the Texas rebels concentrated on killing as many Mexicans as they could. Bowie died fighting from his sickbed. Crockett fell near the end of the five-hour battle. The only survivors were a woman and her 15-month-old baby, along with a few other children and black slaves.

Crazed with hatred of the rebels who had killed so many of their fellow soldiers, the victorious Mexican troops went wild. They mutilated and then burned the bodies of dead rebels.

Santa Anna may have thought that such action would teach a lesson to those still in revolt against his government. He sent a message to Sam Houston, the commander of a rebel army, offering peace and amnesty to all who would lay down their arms and submit to his rule.

However, the defeat at the Alamo and the treatment of its fallen defenders only hardened the resolve of Houston and his troops. On April 21, Houston's army avenged the Alamo at the Battle of San Jacinto by capturing Santa Anna and insuring Texas independence.

*The Civil War was the bloodiest war in American history as brother fought brother and friend fought friend. Capt. James Hope of the 2nd Vermont Militia painted this scene of the First Battle of Bull Run after he participated in the fighting there.*

*After the war, the completion of a transcontinental rail line began changing the face of America forever.*

# CHAPTER 20: CIVIL WAR, RECONSTRUCTION, AND INDIAN WARS

Although the founding of the United States had brought increased rights to many groups, most African Americans continued to be held in bondage as slaves. Their situation was the major factor that sparked the Civil War from 1861 to 1865. However, African Americans themselves had fought in a variety of sometimes subtle and sometimes violent ways for fair treatment and civil rights since their first days in the "New World."

A subtle way in which some blacks resisted slavery was by learning to read and write—skills that were outlawed to them in most of the South. A few slaves were taught by their masters or mistresses. Others learned from white children their own age, whom they bribed with bread and other food. Those slave ministers who were literate smuggled in Bibles and prayer books and organized reading classes among their congregations.

Slaves made their own pens out of oak or hickory sticks. They made ink by cutting *galls*—abnormal growths on oak trees—off the trees and soaking the galls overnight in water. They made paper by cutting sheets of bark from a pine tree and smoothing them out.

*Before the war, abolitionists, such as Sojourner Truth, above, helped blacks escape slavery via the Underground Railroad. After the war, white teachers, one of whom is shown in the 1866 photo at left, came to the South to teach blacks. The students learned quickly, and they filled half of all the South's teaching jobs by 1870.*

243

**S**lave Revolts. In 1800, an African American named Gabriel Prosser, possibly inspired by the revolt led by Toussaint L'Ouverture a few years earlier in what is now Haiti, led a slave revolt in Virginia, intending to make it a state for blacks. Prosser, highly intelligent and a careful planner, was also a devout Christian who had an abiding hatred for the inhumanity of slavery. In the spring and summer of 1800, Prosser, his wife, and his two brothers sought recruits and planned the rebellion. The plotters intended to capture Richmond, the capital of Virginia, seize arms there, and use them against whites.

By August, about 1,000 slaves had pledged their support to Prosser and had hidden away various weapons. On August 30 — the day planned for the uprising — two slaves told authorities about Prosser's plan. That night, a violent thunderstorm flooded the roads and washed out the bridges leading into Richmond, causing a fatal delay for Prosser and his followers. State militia units dispersed the rebels, capturing Prosser and about three dozen others. After a trial, they were executed.

Probably the most well-known attempt at rebellion occurred in Southampton County, Virginia. On the night of Aug. 21, 1831, a black slave and preacher named Nat Turner led a band of rebels to the home of Joseph Travis, Turner's owner. Turner and his followers killed Travis, his wife, two boys, and an infant. Then, traveling across the country still gathering followers, the rebels continued to kill whites as they went. Eventually 60 whites died.

Militiamen and armed white farmers hunted down most of Tur-

*Painted in 1862 by Eastman Johnson, The Ride for Liberty depicts an African American family trying to escape to freedom.*

ner's followers and indiscriminately killed any black who aroused the faintest suspicion. Two months later, Turner was captured. He was tried, found guilty of insurrection, and hanged.

The cotton planters were among the leaders of Southern society, and they believed that slavery was a vital element of the cotton kingdom for its economic survival. Fears of future uprisings led to even further restrictions on slaves' activities, especially when the slaves were not working in the fields. At the same time, any pro-abolition sentiment among the planters disappeared.

# The Underground Railroad.

In the North, however, abolitionist sentiment grew over the years, becoming ever more vocal and insistent. A covert system called the Underground Railroad helped bring black slaves north into freedom. "Conductors" such as Harriet Tubman and Sojourner Truth—former slaves themselves—led small groups of slaves from place to place, usually at night, in a series of small journeys that eventually brought them out of the slave states into the North. Some stops on the Underground Railroad included the homes of abolitionists where there were secret, hidden rooms. The escapees could hide there in relative safety until the next part of the journey began. Eventually, this system helped thousands of African Americans shed bondage and find freedom in the North and in Canada.

# Immigrants and Civil War.

Despite such efforts as the Compromise of 1850, the issues of slavery and states' rights finally split the American union. Eleven Southern states seceded to form the Confederate States of America, and the Civil War began in April 1861.

*Harriet Tubman made 19 "trips" on the Underground Railroad and helped about 300 slaves to escape. She was never caught and never lost a slave on any of the rescue trips.*

The immigrant response to war immediately fell along sectional lines. The Germans, Irish, and others who lived in the South supported the Confederate cause. An exception was a portion of the German immigrant population in East Texas that favored the Union.

Loyalty to either the Union or the Confederacy prompted thousands of immigrants to enlist, though the majority joined the Union forces because most of the more recent immigrants lived in the North. After draft laws were enacted on both sides, the lure of payment to take a draftee's place also played a role. In the North, the offer of immediate citizenship upon honorable discharge enticed many immigrants to enlist. Immigration continued at a high rate throughout the war, and many immigrants joined the Union army as soon as they reached America.

At the start of the war, many immigrants tended to join the Union forces in groups, forming ethnic companies and regiments. For example, the 32nd Indiana, the Ninth Wisconsin, the Ninth Ohio, and the 20th New York were composed mostly of Germans, while a company in the Third Minnesota and one in the 43rd Illinois were made up of Swedes. The 15th Wisconsin was a combined Swedish and Norwegian outfit. The 17th Wisconsin was an Irish regiment, as were regiments from Michigan, New York, Massachusetts, and several other states. Enlistment by ethnic groups occurred less often in the South. In either case, mounting casualties diluted units' ethnic characteristics. When command-

ers needed replacements they took the troops available without regard to national origin.

As the war dragged on, enthusiasm for enlistment flagged, and both sides resorted to *conscription*, the compulsory enlistment of men in the armed forces. Both the Union and Confederate governments' conscription efforts faced opposition, which in many cases included rioting, particularly in the North. Hardly a Northern state escaped the rioting, but the worst occurred in New York City.

The U.S. Congress passed a Conscription Act early in 1863, under which all able-bodied male citizens from ages 20 to 45 as well as male immigrants who had applied for citizenship were enrolled. The drawing for the draft in New York City started on Saturday, July 12, and the names appeared in the Sunday papers.

The drawing resumed on Monday but ended quickly when the building site was set afire by protestors. In addition, the offices of the *New York Tribune* were set afire, as were the homes of prominent citizens who supported Lincoln's war policies, which in-

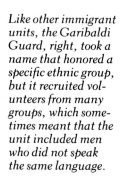

*Like other immigrant units, the Garibaldi Guard, right, took a name that honored a specific ethnic group, but it recruited volunteers from many groups, which sometimes meant that the unit included men who did not speak the same language.*

# OPENING THE WEST: TRAILS AND RAILROADS

On May 10, 1869, the tracks of the Union Pacific Railroad and the Central Pacific Railroad were finally connected at Promontory, Utah.

Portland

Oregon Trail

Central Pacific Railroad

Promontory

Union Pacific

Cheyenne    Railroad

Oregon Trail

Omaha

Sacramento
San Francisco

Independence

Old Spanish Trail

Santa Fe    Trail

Los Angeles

Santa Fe

In the 1850's and 1860's, Scott's Bluff was a major landmark on the Oregon Trail, as shown in this recreation of pioneer life.

*Sgt. William Carney, below, of the all-black 54th Massachusetts Volunteers, was the first of 23 blacks to win the Congressional Medal of Honor during the Civil War.*

*The bravery of the 54th Mass. paved the way for the creation of other all-black units, including the 107th Colored Infantry, shown here, which guarded Washington, D.C.*

cluded freedom for slaves. The New York rioters lynched several blacks by hanging them from lampposts and set fire to an orphanage for African-American children. Conscription also produced another difficult situation by creating drafted men who did not want to serve. However, wealthy men were able to pay poor men—often immigrants—to serve in their place. The substitute clause reminded many, especially the numerous recent Irish immigrants, of their poverty and strongly suggested that the Civil War was a rich man's war and a poor man's fight. It seemed grossly unfair that a man with $300—more than a whole year's wages to thousands of immigrants and other Americans—could buy his way out of the draft by finding a substitute.

The substitution clause was only one reason for immigrant anger about war issues. In addition, a lack of skills forced many immigrants into low-paying menial jobs, such as dockworker and drayman, for which they competed with free African Americans. As a consequence, many immi-grants, especially the newly arrived Irish, opposed emancipation of slaves, viewing it only as an idea that would increase competition for jobs. Emancipation would also deprive the poorest and least-skilled immigrants of the one group that many of them believed stood between them and the very bottom of the heap—black slaves.

For many immigrants, though, the Civil War brought several benefits. Finally, the 30-year splurge of nativism came to a close, and participation in the war gave newcomers a kind of equality with Americans whose roots in the nation ran deeper. The war years were prosperous for some of those in the North who stayed at home, and a few immigrants shared in these economic benefits. In addition, their identification with a nation fighting a crucial war helped soften memories of the world they had left behind. The war did not remove ethnic boundaries and differences by any means, but on the whole it strengthened the ties of recent immigrants to the new homeland.

The end of the Civil War led to the emigration of some 5,000 Southerners to Brazil, then the only nation in the Americas that still tolerated slavery. The Brazilian government encouraged the Confederate emigration by offering long-term loans to pay for passage, land for as little as 22 cents an acre (0.4 hectare), immediate Brazilian citizenship, and exemption from military service.

However, the emigrants—most of whom came from Alabama, Georgia, and Tennessee—found life in their new homeland to be extremely

14th, and 15th amendments to the Constitution. These amendments abolished slavery, gave full citizenship to African Americans, and granted black males the right to vote.

During Reconstruction, many African Americans in the South won election to both state and local offices. Although they achieved some political power, blacks were unable to establish much economic strength. Many were forced into sharecropping for white landowners, which often left them not much better off economically than they had been as slaves.

> . . . units such as the 54th and 55th Massachusetts Volunteers compiled outstanding records as black enlisted men fought for their own freedom through the Union victory.

difficult. The soil was often unproductive for crops, and tropical diseases took a heavy toll on the people. Many emigrants ran short of money. The language barrier was yet another obstacle. As a result, many of the emigrants soon returned to the United States. Those who stayed settled mostly in the town of Americana, where one can still find streets named after such emigrants as Robert Norris and Cicero Jones.

**Blacks and Reconstruction.** About 180,000 African Americans served in the Union armies, and units such as the 54th and 55th Massachusetts Volunteers compiled outstanding records as black enlisted men fought for their own freedom through the Union victory. During and just after the war, states ratified the 13th,

Reconstruction also saw the establishment of secret groups such as the Ku Klux Klan and the Knights of the White Camellia. These groups of whites used intimidation and terror in the South to prevent blacks from voting and from advancing economically and politically. When the last federal troops left the area in 1877, the way was clear for these whites to "redeem" the South. Their efforts led to laws that denied most African-American men the vote and to laws that segregated blacks in almost every aspect of life.

**Exodusters.** Thousands of African Americans responded by leaving the South for the North or the West and becoming so-called "exodusters." John Solomon Lewis, a Louisiana sharecropper, was one example.

In the spring of 1879, Lewis, his wife, and four children hid out in the woods for three weeks until a steamboat heading north on the Mississippi responded to their signal and took them aboard. When they finally reached their destination, Lewis said:

I looked on the ground and I says this is free ground. Then I looked on the heavens, and I says them is free and beautiful heavens. Then I looked within my heart, and I says to myself I wonder why I never was free before? . . .

I asked my wife did she know the ground she stands on. She said "No!"

I said it is free ground; and she cried like a child for joy.

The Lewis' destination was Kansas, where the influx of free blacks from Louisiana, Kentucky, Mississippi, and Tennessee had increased the African-American population almost threefold from 16,250 in the 1870's to 43,100 in the 1880's. Once there, the new residents sometimes settled in established communities and sometimes started new communities of their own. The town of Nicodemus was founded by Kentuckians in 1877 and became the best-known African-American community in Kansas. To blacks, movement to Kansas might have had symbolic overtones. It was there that the first major battles over slavery were fought in the 1850's, and Kansas finally entered the Union as a free state in 1861.

However, African Americans still did not have the same civil rights as whites did. The Civil War and Reconstruction had won many rights for African Americans, but much was left undone. African Americans could not live wherever they pleased, and their children could not attend just any school. Many states segregated school children by race into separate buildings. It was not until 1954 that school segregation was outlawed by the Supreme Court with its landmark decision in the case of *Brown v. Board of Education of Topeka*. The civil rights movement of the 1960's and 1970's continued the effort to achieve full equality for blacks in American society.

*In 1885, the people of Nicodemus, Kan., gathered for this group portrait of themselves and their town. Three years later, the local newspaper, the* Cyclone, *highlighted plans for the upcoming 25th anniversary celebration of the Emancipation Proclamation.*

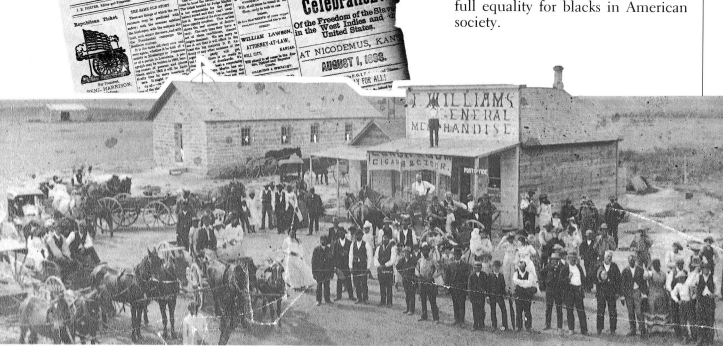

**Indian Wars.** The westward movement of whites as well as blacks led to a time of great wars with the Indians of the area. The government had created the huge Indian Country west of the Mississippi River and had guaranteed that it belonged to the Indians for "as long as the rivers shall run and the grass shall grow." However, pioneers heading west soon began to cast hungry eyes on the land, and then prospectors found both gold and silver in places such as the Black Hills in present-day South Dakota and in Wyoming, where gold was later discovered. Starting in the 1850's, the government began buying back some of the land from the Indians and settling them on reservations throughout the West.

The Plains Indians and others fought to keep their land and avoid being confined to reservations. The 1874 discovery of gold in the Black Hills of South Dakota caused whites to pour into the area held by the Sioux, often disregarding the Indians' rights. Skirmishes broke out, and Brigadier General George Crook ordered the Sioux onto a reservation. Outraged, Chief Sitting Bull declared, "we are an island of Indians in a lake of whites. . . . These soldiers want war. . . . We'll give it to them!" The ensuing battles included the Battle of the Rosebud, "Custer's Last Stand," and finally, in 1890, the Battle of Wounded Knee.

Although the Indians won some battles—as in Custer's Last Stand—they lost all the wars. This was true for the Arapaho, Kiowa, Cheyenne, Modoc, Nez Percé, Ute, Navajo, and Apache, and others. The uprisings lasted for decades, with Apache warriors continuing to fight until 1900, but eventually, the better equipped, more numerous whites won.

*West Point graduate Gen. George Armstrong Custer, top left, and his unit of about 210 soldiers were killed by Indian warriors who used new fighting tactics that they had been given by Sitting Bull, above. The buffalo robe in the center depicts the Indians' victory.*

# PART 8: FROM CIVIL WAR TO WORLD WAR

Between 1861 and 1914, almost 23 million immigrants, mostly from Europe, came to the United States. For many reasons, the arrival of so many immigrants disturbed "native" Americans, and there were numerous efforts to exclude or severely restrict the entry of immigrants considered to be undesirable.

*Arriving in America was a very big event for immigrants. The people who arrived on the* Patricia *in 1906 gathered on the ship's main deck for a photograph to commemorate the event before they disembarked for Ellis Island.*

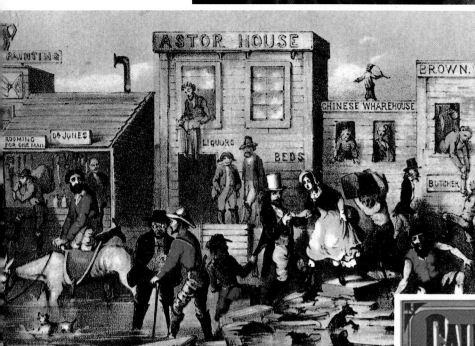

Although rumored to be paved with gold, the streets of San Francisco in the mid-1800's, as shown above, were actually not paved at all. However, advertisements boasting of California's climate were not incorrect.

Weather in New York could be more severe. A snowy Fifth Avenue is shown here in this 1893 Alfred Stieglitz photo.

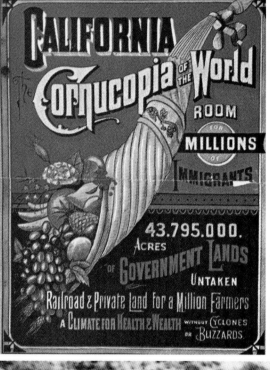

# CHAPTER 21: MORE IMMIGRANTS

An Italian immigrant in the 1800's supposedly said: "I came to America because I heard the streets were paved with gold. When I got here, I found out three things: First, the streets weren't paved with gold; second, they weren't paved at all; and third, I was expected to pave them."

The late 1800's saw a flood of immigrants to America. Most came from Europe, but hundreds of thousands came from Asia as well. As the previously mentioned immigrant said, Italians and other newcomers did play a major role in paving America's streets. Immigrants also mined coal, built railroads, slaughtered cattle, and packed meat. They made clothing and shoes and performed a host of other tasks that contributed to America's growth and productivity.

From colonial times to the Civil War, most immigrants to America came from northern and western Europe. After the Civil War, the immigrants were often from central, southern, and eastern Europe. By the 1890's, the balance had been tipped

*Immigrants, such as this family arriving at Ellis Island about 1910, usually brought only a few articles of clothing and little else with them when they came to America.*

in favor of newcomers from those regions.

**I**talians. Between 1899 and 1910, a total of 2,284,061 immigrants arrived from Italy, 285,371 in 1907 alone. A great many came from the southern part of that country, the majority of them being men between the ages of 16 and 45. Many immigrated with the intention of sending for their families once they had accumulated some money. Others planned on saving money and then returning home with it. About a third of those who arrived before 1920 did go back.

In the cities, Italian immigrants often lived in neighborhoods that came to be called "Little Italys." Many Italian women found work in the garment and paper-flower industries, especially in New York City. Italian men became prominent in construction, which used the *padrone*, or boss, system for many years.

The padrone was someone—usually a man—who spoke both English and Italian and hired workers for temporary jobs in industries that used unskilled labor on short notice for specified time periods. In New York, padrones or their representatives often met immigrants at the dock as they arrived. For a fee, the padrone placed

---

## Between the 1880's and the 1920's, about 1 million Polish immigrants came to America.

---

Italians often settled on the East Coast in New York, New Jersey, and New England. Many also made their way west to cities such as Pittsburgh, Cleveland, and Chicago, and south to New Orleans. In New Orleans, some fished or became dockworkers. Others entered the import-export business and retail merchandising. Many of those who reached San Francisco eventually prospered as fishers, bankers, food processors, and merchants. Although many Italian immigrants had been peasant farmers in their homeland, the price of land and the other expenses of getting into farming in America pushed that work beyond the reach of most. However, some did become truck farmers or worked in the vineyards in California.

the new workers in railroad and building construction and other jobs in various parts of the nation.

For a time, padrones performed a useful function in finding jobs for newly arrived immigrants and helping them learn about the country, but many padrones overcharged, short-changed, and otherwise took advantage of immigrants. As state legislatures enacted restrictions on padrone activities, and as the great flood of immigrants became better acquainted with America, the system gradually died out.

Several times a year, the nation's "Little Italys" were the scene of joyous celebrations of saints' days. Italian immigrants often brought their native costumes with them to the United

States and took great pride in wearing them on such occasions.

One of the most popular saints' days was that of San Gennaro, who was martyred by the Romans in A.D. 306. The celebration took place at night. People strung multicolored electric lights across the neighborhood's main street and set up booths selling candles, candies, and the like on the sidewalks. Then a group of men carried an effigy of San Gennaro up and down the street, with thousands of people following in procession. The celebration was topped off by a fireworks display.

# Poles.
Divided among Prussia, Austria, and Russia in the 1700's, Poland did not exist as a nation again until after World War I ended in 1918.

Although some Poles immigrated to America between 1800 and 1860, a greater influx took place after the Civil War. A desire for farmland of their own was an important reason for Polish immigration, though many of those who left German Poland wished to escape religious troubles as the German government sought to reduce the power of the Roman Catholic Church. The possibility of relatively high wages also lured Poles to America. Between the 1880's and the 1920's, about 1 million Polish immigrants came to America.

Many Polish immigrants settled in New York, Pittsburgh, Milwaukee, Cleveland, and Detroit. By the mid-1880's, Chicago had 40,000 Polish residents and was known as the "American Warsaw." In the cities, Poles worked in steel mills, coal mines, foundries, and oil refineries.

*Many Polish immigrants found employment in factories in cities in the Middle West. These workers were photographed in a Chicago sausage factory in 1909.*

*Greek immigrants often started restaurants, bakeries, and candy stores in the United States. This photograph shows a Greek American named Rose Boosalis, who was the cashier in her family's candy store in Milwaukee, Wis.*

**G**reeks. Beginning in the 1890's, the desire for a better life prompted thousands of Greeks to leave their homeland for the United States. About 300,000 Greek immigrants arrived in America between 1899 and 1914.

Most Greek immigrants settled in cities such as New York and Chicago. At first, many unskilled Greeks relied on a padrone system similar to the Italian one and got temporary jobs on construction gangs, in shoeshine parlors, and in restaurants. Others found steady employment in slaughterhouses, coal mines, textile factories, steel mills, and tanneries. Many started small family-run restaurants where they offered inexpensive food and worked long hours. Other Greeks began their own small businesses, such as shoeshine parlors, flower shops, and candy stores. Like other immigrant groups, Greeks often lived together in their own communities within cities. These communities, often called "Greektowns," usually were centered around a Greek Orthodox church.

**A**rmenians. The first record of an Armenian immigrant is that of someone who arrived in colonial Jamestown in 1618 or 1619. By that time, Armenia was a tiny Christian area that had been taken over by the huge Ottoman Empire, which was Muslim. Most Armenians were poor farmers, but a small group were skilled workers, bankers, or business owners.

In the 1800's, a reawakening of Armenian nationalism led to Ottoman political and economic repression. The result was the loss of property, exile, or death for thousands. In the 1890's, about 2,500 Armenians arrived in the United States. Between 1900 and 1914, some 50,000 more followed. Another 2,500 who had been living under Russian rule had also arrived by 1914.

Armenian immigrants settled in many Eastern and Midwestern states, where they found jobs in iron foundries, steel mills, and textile factories. About 10,000 made their way to California and established themselves in the grape and wine industry there.

Eventually many Armenians set up small businesses, such as grocery stores and carpet shops, or they entered professions such as teaching, engineering, and medicine.

# Hungarians.

In the late 1800's, recruiters for the railroads and other industries found many interested listeners among Hungarians. In Hungary at that time, unskilled labor was paid from 20 to 60 cents per day, depending on an employer's need for workers. By comparison, an unskilled laborer in America could earn more than $2 a day, which seemed like a veritable fortune when viewed from across the Atlantic Ocean.

Among the first Hungarian immigrants to America in the 1800's were those who had participated in the unsuccessful revolution of 1848-1849 that tried to overthrow the Austro-Hungarian monarchy and replace it with a democratic government. Lajos Kossuth, one of the leading revolutionaries, was feted in many places in America when he arrived. Many Hungarian communities in America mourned Kossuth's death in 1894 at age 92 with parades and a period of mourning. His name lives on in the community of Kossuthville, Fla.

Between 1899 and 1914, nearly 460,000 Hungarians entered the United States. Many found work in the coal mines of Pennsylvania, West Virginia, and Illinois, and in steel mills around the country.

# Jews.

The persecution of Jews dates back thousands of years. However, anti-Semitism increased greatly in the 1800's in Europe and was especially harmful in Russia and Russian-held Poland. *Pogroms*—the organized massacre of Jews—were permitted if not directly sponsored by the Czarist government. These horrifying events were frequent and took the lives of thousands. In 1881, the assassination of Czar Alexander II by anarchists led to pogroms against 200 Jewish communities and ushered in a period of intense persecution that lasted for three decades.

However, the pogroms were not the only motive for Jewish immigra-

*Some Armenian immigrants, such as these silk weavers, had marketable skills that helped them get jobs in the United States.*

*Many Jewish immigrants started small businesses on New York City's Lower East Side because of the area's many low-rent tenements. Above, pushcarts line up in front of the shops on Hester Street.*

*The clothing industry was one business that made use of sweatshops, the makeshift factories where poverty-stricken people worked at top speed for 12 or more hours a day in an effort to earn a living wage.*

tion. The growth of large-scale farming in Europe had reduced the opportunities in rural communities for Jewish merchants, traders, and peddlers because they were not allowed to own land. The growth of the factory system also reduced the chances for skilled workers—Jewish and otherwise—to make a living.

In search of safety and a better life, many Jews began fleeing Europe for the United States. By 1880, about 250,000 Jewish immigrants had arrived. Between 1880 and 1914, the number swelled to 2.3 million. They came from Russia, Russian Poland, and several other European countries including Germany, Hungary, Romania, and Austria.

Two-thirds of the Jewish immigrants settled in New York City, Chicago, Philadelphia, and Boston. Most of the rest selected Cleveland, Baltimore, Los Angeles, or Pittsburgh. By 1914, New York City alone had 1.4 million Jewish residents. Like the Greeks and other groups, Jewish immigrants often established their own neighbor-

hoods and communities within larger American cities. Once settled, many Jews worked as artisans, peddlers, small shopkeepers, or factory laborers. They became particularly prominent in the New York garment industry, where at one time a third of all workers were Jewish.

Although they were not persecuted as they had been in Europe, Jewish immigrants certainly did not escape prejudice and discrimination in America, especially as they began to move up the economic ladder. Prejudiced writings and speeches sometimes described Jewish immigrants as determined to take over the nation's commerce, banking, and even the entire country. Jews were barred from living in some apartment buildings and other residential areas, and many social organizations refused to accept them. Help-wanted ads sometimes specified "Christians only." Some colleges and universities established quotas, accepting only a limited number of Jewish applicants. Professional organizations sometimes established quotas, too.

Chinese. The first Chinese to arrive in the United States in sizable numbers were about 25,000 who came seeking gold in California after 1848. However, not unlike the Jews, Chinese immigrants were often barred from the best jobs and certain neighborhoods. In the 1860's, many male Chinese immigrants labored to build the Central Pacific Railroad. Later, Chinese immigrants helped build both the Southern Pacific Railroad and the Northern Pacific Railroad, too.

By 1880, the United States had more than 105,000 Chinese residents. Most lived in California where they worked on vegetable farms, in vineyards, and in orchards where they often made notable contributions. For example, a Chinese farmer named Ah Bing, in Milwaukie, Ore.,

is credited with the development of the bing cherry. Other Chinese became prominent in California factories that produced shoes, clothing, and cigars. Some Chinese entrepreneurs started their own successful factories, while a few managed to buy land and start vegetable farms.

**J**apanese. It is difficult to determine the number of early Japanese immigrants to the United States, because an unknown number arrived and then left, in some instances several times. However, the 1920 census listed 111,010 Japanese-American residents.

Like many other groups, Japanese immigrants came to America to take advantage of the new nation's need for laborers, and they found jobs on railroads, in logging camps, and in the fishing industry. Thousands also became farmworkers on the West Coast, especially in California, and some eventually became owners of those farms. Still others started restaurants,

grocery stores, and rooming houses, which were often family-run enterprises that provided employment for a whole group.

Because most Japanese laborers could not afford to return to Japan to look for wives, they developed the practice of obtaining "picture brides." They would send a photograph of themselves to their ancestral village. There, a Japanese woman would marry the photograph, after which she was eligible to come to the United States to be with her husband.

Many such marriages worked out well. However, in some instances the Japanese laborers sent back pictures taken when they were young. It was quite a shock for a woman of 18 to meet a husband of 50 instead of 23, and so some women returned to Japan on the next boat.

Overall, millions of immigrants from Europe and Asia came to America in the late 1800's in search of better lives for themselves and their children. Many eventually did achieve economic success, but they sometimes found prejudice, too.

*Although most Japanese immigrants lived in California and other western states, a few, such as these Texas rice farmers, migrated to other areas of the country.*

*Many of the immigrants who came through Ellis Island were families with small children.*

*By the early 1900's, many countries required their citizens, including emigrants, to have passports. The one pictured is from Italy.*

# CHAPTER 22: THE PORT

The gigantic Statue of Liberty, officially called *Liberty Enlightening the World*, was designed by the noted French sculptor Frédéric Auguste Bartholdi. Bartholdi selected Bedloe's Island, in Upper New York Bay, as the site for the monument, a gift from the people of France to honor the friendship between their country and the United States.

*The Main Building on Ellis Island was built in the ornate style popular in the late 1800's. The former immigration station at Ellis Island and the Statue of Liberty make up the Statue of Liberty National Monument.*

In December 1883, the Pedestal Fund Committee held an art exhibition and sale to raise money for the statue's pedestal. Poet Emma Lazarus contributed a sonnet for the occasion. She entitled it "The New Colossus," in reference to one of the so-called seven wonders of the ancient world: a huge statue that once towered above the magnificent harbor on the island of Rhodes in the eastern Mediterranean Sea.

Herself a Jew, Lazarus was increasingly concerned about the fate of many European Jews who were then suffering intense persecution, espe-

263

cially in Russia. She saw the Statue of Liberty as a strong symbol of America's status as a refuge for the oppressed everywhere.

The Statue of Liberty became a national monument in 1924. Ironically, that same year, Congress passed the most restrictive immigration legis-

Not like the brazen giant of Greek fame,
With conquering limbs astride from land to land;
Here at our sea-washed, sunset gates shall stand
A mighty woman with a torch, whose flame
Is the imprisoned lightning, and her name Mother of Exiles.
From her beacon-hand
Glows world-wide welcome; her mild eyes command
The air-bridged harbor that twin cities frame.

"Keep, ancient lands, your storied pomp!"
    cries she
With silent lips. "Give me your tired, your poor,
Your huddled masses yearning to breathe free,
The wretched refuse of your teeming shore.
Send these, the homeless, tempest-tost to me,
I lift my lamp beside the golden door!"

*Emma Lazarus.*

The necessary funds for constructing the pedestal were finally raised, in large part due to the fund-raising campaign of *The World*, a New York newspaper. The pedestal was finished in April 1886. On Oct. 28 of that year, when the statue was dedicated, boats filled the harbor and New York City celebrated with a great parade. President Grover Cleveland and his Cabinet were there, along with French officials and the statue's sculptor, Frédéric Auguste Bartholdi.

# The First Century.

Speakers at the dedication hailed the statue as a symbol of international peace and friendship. They said "Miss Liberty" represented America as a shining and encouraging example of freedom and democracy in the world. In 1903, a New York friend of Emma Lazarus' got permission to put a bronze tablet inscribed with the lines of her poem "The New Colossus" on the huge statue's pedestal.

lation in the nation's history.

As refugees streamed out of Europe in the 1930's, *Liberty Enlightening the World* grew even more important as a symbol of refuge from oppression. The importance of that symbolism continued to grow during and after World War II. However, age and pollution took a heavy toll on the statue. Finally, a major restoration was undertaken. On July 4, 1986, Americans across the nation celebrated the rededication of this great immigrant landmark.

# Ellis Island.

Also standing in New York Harbor is Ellis Island, the processing center through which passed millions of immigrants. Beginning in 1892 and for several decades thereafter, between 70 and 75 per cent of all immigrants entered America through Ellis Island. The procedure was hectic, sometimes terrifying, and occasionally humorous.

In 1855, New York State immigration officials opened Castle Garden on the southern tip of Manhattan Island as a processing center for new arrivals. Castle Garden was originally a fort in the War of 1812. Later it became a theater and an amusement park. Eventually, the huge number of immigrants overtaxed the facility. In addition, the federal government assumed jurisdiction over all immigration. These events led to the opening of Ellis Island in 1892. Built on a small piece of land in the harbor, the island was enlarged to 27.5 acres (11 hectares) by the use of landfill. The facilities included waiting rooms, examination rooms, a hospital, dining rooms, and administration offices.

Immigrants who were processed through Ellis Island had crossed the ocean in steerage class. Steerage was originally that portion of a ship below the decks and near the rudder and other parts of the steering apparatus. By the late 1800's, steerage on passenger ships offered somewhat better accommodations than those experienced by earlier travelers, and most voyages took only 10 to 12 days. Still, a fare of anywhere from $12 to $30— depending on the ship—often bought little more than a bumpy mattress in a narrow, overcrowded, poorly ventilated space that was usually below the water line.

Not all immigrants, though, belonged to the "huddled masses" who had to scrimp to save even the low fare for a steerage-class passage. Newcomers with first- and second-class accommodations did not pass through Ellis

*The Great Hall of Ellis Island's Main Building was where families would wait their turn for examination and entry into America.*

*In 1876, parts of the uncompleted Statue of Liberty became a tourist sensation. For a small fee that helped pay for the statue's pedestal, people could buy tickets and climb into the torch.*

*In the peak year of 1907, as many as 3,000 people a day were processed through Ellis Island.*

*The huge number of immigrants meant that medical tests on Ellis Island were very brief.*

from one processing stage to another and acted as go-betweens during the medical examinations. U.S. law forbade the entry of persons afflicted with "loathesome" diseases such as leprosy, tuberculosis, ringworm, or trachoma.

The medical examinations, conducted by physicians highly skilled in quick diagnosis, were crucial. Many immigrants went through these examinations without even realizing it. The first exam was when a medical team watched the immigrants climbing stairs, walking, and resting. The team's job was to look for obvious signs of mental or physical disease or disability. The next medical team looked for evidence of specific diseases and for signs of lice. Other doctors listened to hearts and lungs. The final team asked immigrants to read an eye chart and searched for signs of a highly contagious eye disease called trachoma through a painful examination that used a buttonhook to roll back the eyelid.

Examiners identified any person with a health problem by writing a letter in chalk on the immigrant's right shoulder. For example, the letter B stood for back problems, C for conjunctivitis, L for lameness, and Ct for trachoma. An X indicated mental retardation, and an X in a circle indi-

Island. Immigration officials boarded the ships and processed those wealthier passengers there. After admission, they were free to proceed to their destinations.

**E**xaminations. Transported by barge and ferryboat to Ellis Island, steerage passengers faced a swift but harrowing experience. Even those with little need to fear failure felt some apprehension as they lined up for the examinations required for entrance into the United States.

Ellis Island employed many interpreters, some of whom spoke half a dozen languages. The interpreters herded the immigrants in groups of 30

*The average length of a personal interview on Ellis Island was about two minutes. After the interview, a few people, such as this boy, were examined more extensively.*

cated severe mental problems. However, except for a few diseases, these diagnoses were often arbitrary, and never before had they been grounds for restriction.

The medical examinations separated immigrants into two groups. One group was made up of people who required further examination and would be turned away if they failed to pass. The other group of immigrants now faced the final hurdle — a series of questions from immigration officers.

The questions were basically simple and designed to make sure that immigrants had at least a little money, would have help in finding jobs so as not to become public charges, had the name and address of a friend or relative, and were neither anarchists nor polygamists — two undesirable types to which federal law denied entry.

Proof of a destination was usually not difficult to produce either, though deciphering the name of a place sometimes spelled phonetically on a smudged piece of paper could challenge an officer's imagination. The destinations included Chikaigo, Neihork Nugers, Deas Moyness Yova, and Linkinbra, which, of course, turned out to be Chicago; Newark, New Jersey; Des Moines, Iowa; and Lincoln, Nebraska.

Since many immigrants were illiterate, examiners used special tests to determine intelligence. One such test consisted of a set of wooden blocks, each bearing a face with a slightly different expression. The immigrant was asked to put the faces with similar expressions together. Another test required immigrants to draw a diamond. Peasants who had never before held a pencil in their hand naturally

*Ellis Island had a playground for immigrant children. They could play while their parents were being questioned and examined.*

found this very difficult. Last of all came a verbal test. The story is told that one inspector asked, "How do you wash stairs, from the top or from the bottom?" The immigrant replied, "I didn't come to America to wash stairs."

Once the final examiner was satisfied, the immigrant received a card of admission and was free to go. Ferries took immigrants from Ellis Island to New York or to New Jersey. Those who were traveling to other places boarded trains for their destinations.

Only about 3 per cent of all immigrants failed to pass the tests on Ellis Island. However, such failures were agonizing, for they meant an end to dreams, and in many cases broke up families.

Between 1892 and 1924, more than 12 million immigrants passed through the Ellis Island reception center. By 1932, however, the huge flow of immigrants had declined to a mere trickle of 21,500 per year. The facility's use as an immigration center was ended soon thereafter.

For decades, Ellis Island sat abandoned. Then in 1974, Dr. Peter Sammartino, the former chancellor of Fairleigh Dickinson University, formed the Restore Ellis Island Committee and brought the plight of the national landmark to the attention of the country. In January 1976, President Gerald Ford signed a bill authorizing the use of $1 million to restore the island. However, it soon became evident to Philip Lax, who had succeeded Sammartino, and others that a different system and much greater funding was needed. In 1980, an agreement was signed with the National Park Service that gave the Ellis Island Restoration Commission the responsibility to raise the necessary funds through private donations.

One of the goals of the Commission is to establish the Family History Center at Ellis Island. Due to be completed in 1992, the center will have a computerized data bank on all the people who passed through the immigration point. With only an immigrant's name to go by, computers will be able to report the name of the ship used for transportation, the day and time the immigrant arrived, the person's health, the names of any traveling companions, how much money the immigrant had, and several other details. Then, the descendants of these immigrants will be able to look into their own pasts in a way not possible before.

# Angel Island.

Although most immigrants between 1861 and 1914 entered the United States through Ellis Island, about 175,000 came through the immigration station at Angel Island in San Francisco Bay. Most of these were Chinese, and they were able to enter the country despite the Chinese Exclusion Act of 1882 because of the 1906 San Francisco earthquake. The quake destroyed the city's records of Chinese businesses and births. As a result, Chinatown residents presented claims for fictitious children in China. Thus, entire villages of "paper sons and daughters" were allowed to come to the United States.

However, their passage through Angel Island was long and unpleasant. Upon arrival, men and women—even from the same family—were separated and put in rooms stacked three to five bunks high. They could go outdoors only twice a day for 15 minutes at a time—into a small yard surrounded by barbed wire. The detention period usually lasted from six months to a year.

Although most of the Chinese were eventually admitted, a substantial number were returned to their homeland. Some—mostly women—committed suicide rather than be deported. The reason was that they had either borrowed or stolen their passage money, and the only course open to them if they were deported was prostitution.

*Immigrants from Asia usually passed through Angel Island in San Francisco Bay.*

On Sept. 9, 1990, the gateway to America for millions of immigrants reopened as the Ellis Island Immigration Museum. Largely inactive for more than 60 years,

limestone Main Building is the only one open to visitors. However, other buildings on the island include the hospital, dormitories, powerhouse, and administrative

building through an orientation area on the first floor, just as the immigrants did.

The first floor now contains one of the four permanent exhibitions. Entitled

"The Peopling of America," it includes a huge globe that lights up to show major immigration routes to America. A movie theater, restaurant, and gift shop are also located on the first floor.

To reach the second floor, visitors can climb the stairs, ride an escalator, or if they are handicapped, use an elevator. Of course, the millions of would-be Americans from 1892 to 1924 had no such choices.

It is on the second floor that visitors encounter the emotional core of Ellis Island—the Great Hall. The large room has an extraordinary tiled and vaulted ceiling

# THE RESTORATION OF ELLIS ISLAND

The only modern addition to the Main Building, above, is a canopy at the front door. At right is the Great Hall during renovation.

the island in New York Harbor had fallen into an almost unrecoverable state. Its restoration, all privately funded, cost about $156 million.

Actually, just part of Ellis Island has been restored. The red brick and

offices. Relatively few immigrants ever entered these facilities. For most immigrants the Main Building *was* Ellis Island.

Today, the Main Building houses the Ellis Island Immigration Museum. Visitors enter the

but no exhibits. In fact, the room where crowds of anxious immigrants once jostled each other is now completely empty except for some of the original benches.

Also on the second floor are two major exhibits. An exhibit called "Peak Immigration Years: 1880-1924" uses a variety of artifacts to trace the immigrant experience from leaving home to resettling in America. The second exhibit, called "Through America's Gate," focuses on the Ellis Island screening process. It includes a restored Board of Special Inquiry Room—the place where officials decided the fates of those who had not passed the initial inspection.

On the third and top floor of the Main Building is a restored dormitory. It was used as a temporary residence for people who did not receive immediate entry into the United States. An exhibit here is called "Treasures from Home." It includes items that immigrants brought with them, a discussion of the restoration of Ellis Island, and a library and oral history studio where people can do immigration research.

That the Main Building has been so beautifully restored is a tribute to the Ellis Island Restoration Commission and its president, Philip Lax, who has devoted almost 15 years of volunteer work to the project. Lax, a successful land developer and interior designer, has a special interest in the project since both of his parents entered America through Ellis Island in the 1920's.

Now it is hoped that the restoration of Ellis Island will fulfill a yearning in millions of Americans to discover what their ancestors endured in search of a new life in a new land.

*Many immigrants in New York City, such as this wistful child, lived in tenements with rickety construction, poor plumbing, and little light.*

*Immigrant children often went to work at very young ages. In 1896, this little girl was photographed selling newspapers in front of New York's City Hall.*

# CHAPTER 23: LIFE IN NEW YORK CITY

Comedian Harpo Marx grew up in New York City in the late 1800's. Many years later, in his autobiography, Marx recalled how the boundaries between immigrant neighborhoods in the city of his youth were often as fixed and as forbidding as any between sovereign nations:

Life in the streets was a tremendous obstacle course for an undersized kid like me. The toughest obstacles were kids of other nationalities. The upper East Side was subdivided into Jewish blocks (the smallest area), Irish blocks, and German blocks, with a couple of Independ-

Immigrant neighborhoods in New York City were usually busy, noisy places that seemed to offer little hope to many of their inhabitants. Among those who did go on to a better economic life were the Marx brothers—Harpo, Gummo, Chico, and Groucho.

ent Italian states thrown in for good measure. That is, the cross streets were subdivided. The north-and-south Avenues—First, Second, Third and Lexington—belonged more to the city than the neighborhood. They were neutral zones. But there was open season on strangers in the cross streets.

If you were caught trying to sneak through a foreign block, the first thing the Irishers or Germans would ask was, "Hey, kid! What Streeter?" I learned it saved time and trouble to tell the truth. I was a 93rd Streeter, I would confess.

"Yeah? What block 93rd Streeter?"

"Ninety-third between Third and Lex." That pinned me down. I was a Jew.

The worst thing you could do was run from Other Street-

*Hester Street was in the heart of New York City's immigrant neighborhood.*

ers. But if you didn't have anything to fork over for ransom you were just as dead. I learned never to leave my block without some kind of boodle in my pocket—a dead tennis ball, an empty thread spool, a penny, anything. It didn't cost much to buy your freedom; the gesture was the important thing.

It was all part of the endless fight for recognition of foreigners in the process of becoming Americans.

**Neighborhoods.** Although New York's immigrant neighborhoods may have been among the toughest and most crowded, in many ways they were not all that different from those found in other large cities across the nation. By the early 1900's, New York City had 340,000 Italian residents, which was nearly 60,000 more than the city of Genoa in Italy itself. In addition, New York had 324,000 Germans and 270,000 people of Irish descent. By comparison the city of Dublin, Ireland, had less than 100,000 more. In New York and other large cities, many of these immigrants tried to make their new neighborhoods a reflection of their old homelands as much as they could by choosing to live together in ethnic neighborhoods that often took up a city block or more. Italian, German, Polish, Irish, Chinese, Hungarian, and Jewish immigrants often lived in such neighborhoods. There were also neighborhood subdivisions of German, Russian, and Polish Jews; northern and southern Italians and Sicilians; Protestant and Catholic Germans; Catholic and Protestant Irish; and other immigrants. The New York neighborhoods became so well established that sightseeing tours visited the areas to show off these seemingly quaint and picturesque recreations of foreign lands. At least many tourists thought the neighborhoods were quaint and picturesque until gangs of small boys occasionally pelted the tour buses with rotten fruit, garbage, and sometimes even dead cats. The immigrants themselves treasured their neighborhoods, but they often found the living conditions something less than charming.

Despite the efforts of many workers, some streets were unpaved and became ribbons of mud during rainy weather. However, muddy or not, by day the streets were hubbubs of noise and congestion. From their push carts, vendors hawked cheeses, pickles, sausages, fruits, eggs, vegetables, fish, chickens, bread, glassware, shoes, stockings, underwear, pots and pans, scissors, ribbon, religious goods, and a host of other items. Since the crowded neighborhoods rarely had any park or yard space, children played in the streets, squealing and shouting at their games of hopscotch, marbles, jacks, and baseball. Merchants and suppliers moved their wares on horses and wagons. Mothers, often carrying or pushing in baby carriages a young child or two, did their daily shopping in an atmosphere that often resembled bedlam.

Immigrant children tried to enjoy whatever they could get "for free." If they were literate, they took advantage of the city's libraries, reading books that took them away from the world around them. They fished for pennies through the grates at sidewalk corners. Like thousands of other New Yorkers, they attended free concerts in Central Park, went picnicking in Prospect Park, and sometimes hiked from one end of Manhattan to the other just to see the sights of the city. Best of all was watching a Fifth Avenue parade with its colorful floats.

*When many people had to live crowded into small apartments, the children often had little room in which to play. In the summer time, they often sought any outdoor "playground" they could find, including fire escapes.*

*Immigrant families were often forced to live in tiny apartments in run-down buildings.*

enements. Since most immigrants were at the bottom of the economic ladder, they had little choice in housing. Some found lodging in large houses that had been subdivided into tiny apartments, often consisting of only a single room. However, the most common type of tenement housing in New York City was the so-called "dumbbell" apartment building. The name came from the building's resemblance to a dumbbell since it was constructed in a shape that looked like two square knobs separated by an indented center structure. However, the indentation was usually just 5 feet (1.5 meters) wide and 2.5 feet (0.76 meters) long. In rows of dumbbell tenements, the indentations formed tiny air and light shafts.

As many as 10 dumbbell tenements lined the side of an average city block. Each building was usually 6 to 8 stories high and about 20 feet (6 meters) wide along the street and 90 feet (27.5 meters) deep. A narrow stairway in the center of the building provided access to the upper floors. There were no elevators.

Dumbbell tenements usually had four apartments of four rooms each on a floor. As many as 250 people might live in one building, jamming several thousand people together in a single block. By 1900, about a third of New York City's population of a little more than 3 million lived in 43,000 tenements, many of them dumbbells.

The narrow air shafts provided little light in the apartments, which reeked with unpleasant odors, especially during humid summer days. As the tenants came and went, and the landlords failed to maintain the buildings, the tenements became more and more run-down. The wallpaper was streaked and torn, and ceilings and walls became dingy from the smoke of coalburning stoves and kerosene lamps. Many tenements were terrible firetraps, as demonstrated all too clearly by the frequent fires in immigrant neighborhoods. In many buildings, the only source of water was a communal pump or faucet—one to a floor. Rows of privies in the courtyards served as toilet facilities. Rats were everywhere, and disease was endemic. In one tenement district, 6 out of every 10 babies died before they reached their first birthdays—an astonishing mortality rate.

**Immigrant Labor.** Such was the housing to which hundreds of thousands of immigrants came home each night, after working 12 hours or longer. Many men paved streets, laid gas pipes, telephone and electrical cables, dug New York's subway tunnels, and built bridges and skyscrapers. Others worked in textile, shoe, glass, and other factories. For these strenuous labors, they often earned little more than $2 a day.

Women and children worked in factories, too. In many cases, women and children labored in sweatshops, often located in the tenements in which they lived. Sweatshop labor sustained the "needle trades," producing clothing of all sorts, along with gloves, hats, lace, and garters. Sweatshop labor was vital to companies making artificial flowers, shelled nuts, and cigars, too. Women also took in boarders, whom they cooked and cleaned for.

Competition in the garment industry was keen, and it kept prices low. Since there was an abundance of labor, though, employers could "sweat" their workers with piecework pay. For example, a worker might be paid just one penny for making seven dozen artificial roses, little more for making a lady's blouse. Usually only utter fatigue brought the workday to an end. However, even by putting in 14 or more hours a day, artificial flower makers and garment workers earned scarcely $200 a year.

*Sweatshops often employed women, because women were not eligible for the somewhat better paying jobs in the building and construction trades that were available to men.*

*Children sometimes worked for pennies, carrying semi-completed clothing from one work site to another.*

*Shocked police officials, above, examine the bodies of some of the victims of the Triangle Shirtwaist fire. At right, fire fighters pour water on the blaze.*

As well as low pay, workers could count on periodic layoffs due to overproduction or other factors. Working only 40 weeks per year was common in the textile industry, while many railroad workers found employment for fewer than 200 days annually.

In 1910, a calculation set $900 as the minimum income a family of five needed to live decently. However, only one in seven foreign-born families met that standard. In today's parlance, most immigrant families lived below the poverty level.

# Hazards in the Workplace.

In addition to receiving such low wages, many workers labored in unhealthy and unsafe conditions. Crippling and deadly industrial accidents were common. For example, dust that clogged the air in textile mills was responsible for lung problems and shortened the lives of many workers. Other industries were hardly better. In 1910, for example, about 3,000 railroad workers were killed on the job and more than 95,000 injured.

Fire was a constant hazard. In March 1911, the worst factory fire in New York City's history swept the Triangle Shirtwaist Company, a clothing company that employed mostly women. The fire broke out on the eighth floor of a 10-story building, and it quickly spread through piles of fabric stacked on the floor. Many employees escaped, but many others were trapped because the single fire escape from the eighth floor was blocked. Panicked workers, some in flames, jumped from window ledges, their bodies piling up on the street below. The tragedy was compounded by the facts that fire department ladders only reached to the seventh floor and safety nets proved too weak to hold victims leaping from such a great

*George Gershwin lived on 72nd Street in New York City after he had become a wealthy and famous composer.*

height. Nearly 150 workers—most of them young women—died that day. More than a third of the deaths were caused by injuries received from jumping.

On April 5—less than two weeks after the Triangle Shirtwaist Company fire—about 120,000 men, women, and children marched through the rain in a memorial parade for the fire's victims. The marchers walked silently, carrying placards that read: "We demand Fire Protection." About 400,000 spectators lined Fifth Avenue. As a result of the parade and various union protest meetings held throughout the city, the New York State Legislature began a four-year investigation that resulted in the passage of several factory safety laws. However, the owners of the Triangle Shirtwaist Company—who were tried on charges of manslaughter—were found not guilty.

Life in the noisy city was a far cry from the quiet, relatively simple village life many immigrants had known. In the past, the changing seasons dictated the tasks at hand, and there was leisure for weddings, christenings, and other celebrations in the midst of a helping, extended family and well-known neighbors. In the cities of America, money was needed to survive. Earning the essential money usually meant long hours on tedious, often debilitating jobs, often without regard for health or the changing seasons. Long work weeks left little time for leisure or reflection on old ways. Each year, a few hundred immigrants gave up and returned home. Many, however, could not afford the return passage.

Most immigrants hoped that their children, by obtaining an education, learning a skill, or making use of a talent might know better lives. Harpo and the other sons of Minnie and Frenchie Marx were among those who did. Other immigrant offspring who became famous in the entertainment world included Harry Houdini, the magician and escape artist who was born of Hungarian parents, and composer George Gershwin and his lyricist brother, Ira, who were the sons of Russian Jews.

Spectacular success stories, however, were the exception rather than the rule. Most immigrant families struggled for two or three generations before escaping the poverty of their immigrant ancestors. Other families never reached that goal.

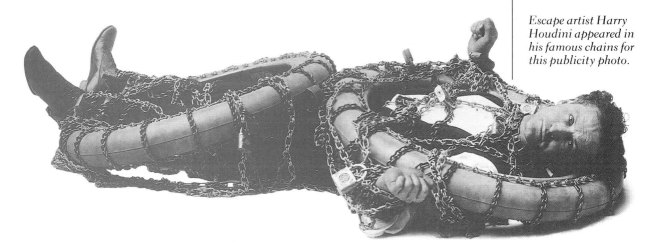

*Escape artist Harry Houdini appeared in his famous chains for this publicity photo.*

*The public school system was one way that many immigrants learned about their new homeland. Textbooks of the era used everyday items, such as dimes and nickels, to teach basic concepts, and students everywhere learned to recite the Pledge of Allegiance.*

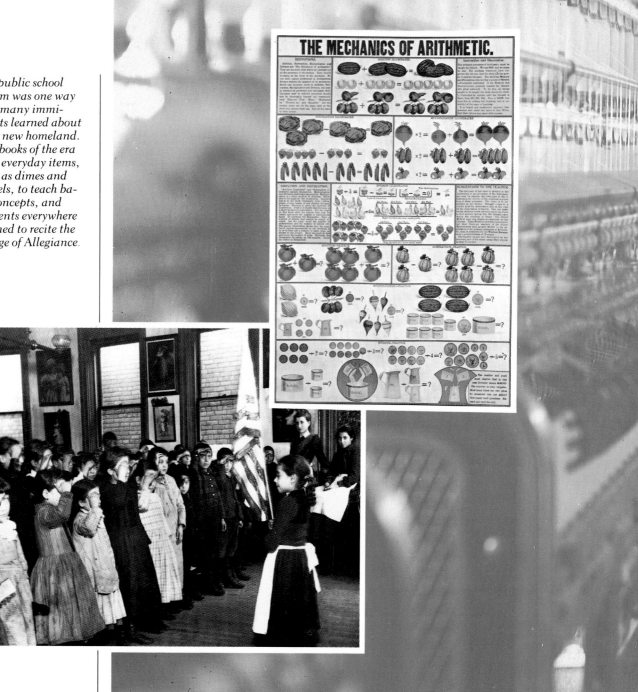

# CHAPTER 24: AID AND AMERICANIZATION

In 1892, America observed the 400th anniversary of Columbus' arrival in the "New World." To mark the occasion, a magazine called *The Youth's Companion* published a solemn pledge of loyalty to the United States, and it quickly gained acceptance in schools across the nation.

Before long, classrooms everywhere began the day with students standing, facing the flag, and reciting the pledge, which in its present-day form is:

*Family finances often meant that children, such as this little factory worker, had to forego an education. People such as Jane Addams, shown here with a Hull House child, helped immigrants get a chance for a better life.*

I pledge allegiance to the flag of the United States of America, and to the Republic for which it stands, one Nation, under God, indivisible, with liberty and justice for all.

Reciting the Pledge of Allegiance was one way to instill patriotism—a goal of schooling—in both immigrants and native-born Americans. There were other ways, too.

**The School Curriculum.** In school, students studied the government, literature, and history of the nation, paying particular attention to the American heroes of the past. Schoolchildren learned how George Washington, the wise and patient "Father of Our Country," led Americans to independence and that he never told a lie. They learned about Honest Abe, who once walked several miles to return a penny and who later saved the Union and freed the slaves. Students presented historical pageants, depicting the first Thanksgiving, American soldiers at Valley Forge, and the winning of the West. No national holiday passed without some form of recognition, be it a story, poem, or pageant.

None of these activities were aimed especially at immigrants. Yet immigrant children learned English, studied the history of their adopted homeland, and observed national holidays, which, taken altogether, could not help but have somewhat of an "Americanizing" effect on them.

In addition to schooling, another means of Americanization—at least for Jewish immigrants—was a column in the *Jewish Daily Forward*, a Yiddish newspaper published in New York City. The column was called A *Bintel Brief*, and it contained letters to the editor and their replies. The letters talked about the various problems the immigrants confronted in their new homeland. Among the topics were: What should a religiously observant Jew do about working on the Sabbath, which in Judaism is Saturday? Should a schoolgirl speak Yiddish or English to her parents? Should a schoolboy try to attend college or go to work to support his mother? Should a Jew say he was a Christian in order to get a job? And so on.

*This class picture from the early 1900's is clear evidence that America's public schools brought together many different immigrant groups.*

At the turn of the century, elementary school classes in Maine not only stressed the importance of reading but also the value of physical exercise.

Schooling also sometimes caused strained relationships between first- and second-generation immigrants, even among groups that recognized education as the primary means for their children to achieve a better life. Immigrant parents often preserved aspects of their native culture in the face of the new and sometimes frightening society they encountered in America. Immigrant children, however, often actively pursued all the new society's ways in an effort to fit in with their new surroundings. In school, immigrants learned the language of America and its national customs and beliefs—customs and beliefs that often clashed with those of their parents and the old homeland. For example, when immigrant children reached marriageable age, they often decided to choose their own spouses rather than allow their parents to select partners for them in the traditional way.

*Many immigrant children had to go to work at very young ages. Some were orphans, but most were from poor families who needed the tiny incomes the children provided. These small workers were usually recruited to do jobs that adults could not—or would not—do. The growth of the textile industry in America depended heavily on the labor of children, such as these two girls. Young boys were often employed in coal mines because they could fit into spaces too small to hold adults.*

# Child Labor.

Although many immigrant groups placed a high value on education, economic realities often demanded that children leave school and work to help supplement a family's income. At the turn of the century, hundreds of thousands of children as young as ten worked at a variety of jobs. They worked in sweatshops, textile factories, coal mines, and glassworks, to name just a few. By 1890, nearly 20 per cent of the nation's children were employed fulltime, usually at wages even lower than those paid to women. Certainly, not all these children were immigrants, but many of them were. It was well into the 1900's before state and national laws regulating child labor and school attendance meant that almost all children remained in school until at least age 16.

# Parochial Schools.

By 1900, about 854,000 children attended parochial schools nationwide. Most of these schools were sponsored and operated by the Roman Catholic Church. In addition, quite a few schools were run by the Lutheran Church or other Protestant denominations. Religious instruction, of course, was the principal rationale for a parochial school education. However, some parochial schools tended to stress "Old World" cultures and offered instruction in the language of the ethnic group involved. To parents who found America to be threatening and believed their own culture was better, stress on "Old World" ways must have seemed comforting. Over the years, though, the emphasis on these ways gradually faded in these schools as both teachers and students became more and more accustomed to American ways.

# Clubs and Societies.

Nearly every immigrant group had its own society, lodge, or cultural group. Many of

*Danish immigrant and social reformer Jacob Riis became well known for his photographs of America's immigrant poor, such as this young boy. Riis' pictures and books helped bring about stricter laws concerning education and child labor.*

these were organized to help keep traditional ways alive, but in many cases, the groups also stood ready to lend a helping hand to new arrivals. There were, for example, the Greek Panhellenic Union, the Hebrew Immigrant Aid Society, the National Council of Jewish Women, the Irish Benevolent Association, and the Deutsch-Amerikanischer National-bund, along with German marching bands, Irish dancing clubs, and many others.

However, not all members of an ethnic group necessarily agreed with one another, and some members established organizations with diametrically opposed aims. For example, the Polish National Alliance, or PNA, stressed acculturation into American society while also recognizing the value of tradition. It offered aid to new immigrants, published newsletters, offered inexpensive insurance policies, organized libraries, set up youth programs, and lobbied for the erection of monuments to Polish heroes such as Thaddeus Kosciuszko and Casimir Pulaski. The Polish Roman Catholic Union, on the other hand, emphasized religious values and Polish separatism and culture.

*In the early 1900's immigrants organized a variety of social groups, such as the Czech physical fitness club shown below.*

## Settlement Houses and the YMCA.

Settlement houses, pioneered by Jane Addams and Ellen Gates Starr at Hull House in Chicago, aided the urban poor in general and immigrants in particular. By 1900, there were more than 100 settlement houses throughout the nation. Together, they offered a wide variety of classes in such things as the English language, cooking, sewing, health, hygiene, and child care.

The Young Men's Christian Association (YMCA) also aided immigrants across the country. For example, many YMCA's conducted English-language and citizenship classes and helped immigrants prepare for citizenship in other ways.

*Music was among the subjects taught at Hull House, which first occupied a dilapidated mansion originally owned by Charles J. Hull, a Chicago businessman. By 1907, the settlement had 12 new buildings and covered a whole city block.*

## Politics and Immigrants.

Politicians, particularly Democrats, often contended that they did more for immigrants than any social agency, and in a way, perhaps they were right. Certainly many immigrants learned some basic lessons from politicians about the realities of party loyalty, and the parties provided critical services—often without patronizing immigrant values and cultures.

As they had for decades near Election Day, precinct workers often met immigrant ships, shepherded the newcomers to friendly judges who quickly granted citizenship, and then saw to it that the new citizens appeared at polling places to scratch X's in the proper columns. Especially in the cities, immigrants—like many others—soon learned to vote for their precinct captain's choices on the ballot.

The political machines remained loyal to the immigrants in return. Precinct workers delivered baskets of food at Thanksgiving and at Christmas. They put in a good word with ward leaders for those in need of jobs, delivered buckets of coal and other necessities when needed, and were prepared to help in times of distress and misfortune. George Washington Plunkitt, a member of New York City's Tammany Hall Democratic organization, put it this way:

What tells in holdin' your grip on your district is to go right down among the poor families and help them in the different ways they need help. . . . If there's a fire . . . for example, any hour of the day or night, I'm usually there with some of my election district captains as soon as the fire engines. If a family is burned out, I don't ask whether they are Republicans or Democrats, and I don't refer them to the Charity Organization Society, which would investigate their case in a month or two and decide they were worthy of help about the time they are dead from starvation. I just get quarters for them, buy clothes for them if their clothes were burned up, and fix them up till they get things runnin' again. It's philanthropy, but its politics, too—mighty good politics. . . . The poor are the most grateful in the world, and, let me tell you, they have more friends in their neighborhoods than the rich have in theirs. . . . The consequence is that the poor look up to George W. Plunkitt as a father, come to him in trouble—and don't forget him on election day.

Tammany Hall, formally called the Society of Tammany, was founded in 1789. The organization's name came from a legendary chief of the Delaware Indians who supposedly welcomed William Penn when he arrived in the "New World." At first, Tammany was a fraternal organization, dedicated mostly to having fun, with a little charitable work thrown in. Members paraded twice a year—on the Fourth of July and on Tammany Day (May 12)—dressed in Indian costumes, with painted faces and carrying tomahawks and bows and arrows. The headquarters of the Society was called The Wigwam, and

Tammany members gave mock-Indian names to the "moons," or months of the year.

Gradually, however, Tammany changed in nature and became a political organization. In 1809, it nominated its first Irish Catholic candidate for public office. However, it was not until the requirement of being a taxpayer in order to vote was removed in 1826 that large numbers of Irish Catholic immigrants became active in Tammany. By the mid-1830's, they made up a large part not only of its membership but of its leadership as well.

*The Society of Tammany got its popular name—Tammany Hall—from the name of its headquarters building, located at 331 Madison Avenue, New York City.*

The late 1800's and early 1900's saw a rise in anti-immigration fervor against the Chinese, shown above, and others. In 1891, an American cartoon blamed all the nation's problems on unrestricted immigration. After San Francisco's 1906 earthquake, shown here, city leaders tried to segregate Chinese and Japanese children in separate schools when the buildings were rebuilt.

# CHAPTER 25: RESTRICTION BEGINS

As the number of Chinese immigrants increased, so did American prejudice against them. The Chinese became the victims of malicious persecution, and Chinese men were sometimes chased by bullies who cut off their long hair braids called *queues*. Then in the 1870's, the Chinese also became the first group to experience exclusion from the United States as the American nativist movement regained strength.

# Chinese Immigration

**C**hinese Immigration. Despite Chinese contributions to American railroad building, mining, and business, white workers found a major fault with Chinese—they kept on coming to America. There were about 63,000 Chinese immigrants by 1870, and approximately 123,000 more arrived during the 1880's.

In 1871, hostility toward the Chinese turned violent on the West Coast. Eighteen Chinese were killed in Los Angeles, and in 1877, some 25 Chinese laundries in San Francisco were burned to the ground. An economic depression had engulfed the country since 1873, and there had been bloody strikes over wage cuts, as well as considerable unemployment. Jobless whites in California made the

*The late 1800's was a time when some immigrant groups tried to restrict the entry of other groups. Denis Kearney, himself a recent immigrant, founded a group in California that urged the government to limit Chinese immigration.*

Chinese a scapegoat on which to blame their misery. All these whites lacked was leadership, which was soon supplied by Denis Kearney, a recently naturalized Irish immigrant who founded the Workingmen's Party in California. Claiming that Chinese laborers worked for wages that were too low and they often served as strikebreakers, Kearney declared that the Chinese must go.

California labor leaders and other lobbyists persuaded people in Congress to introduce legislation that would limit Chinese immigration. In 1879, a bill prohibiting ships from carrying more than 15 Chinese to the United States at a time passed easily. However, the bill conflicted with an earlier treaty with China that recognized the right of emigrants from that nation to enter the United States, so President Rutherford B. Hayes vetoed the bill. Nevertheless, the stage for exclusion had now been set.

# Exclusion.

A new treaty signed in 1880 modified the 1868 agreement

*The two I.D.s at right describe their owners as "merchants." The Chinese Exclusion Act, designed to bar Chinese immigration, contained a loophole that allowed merchants, teachers, students, and travelers to enter the country.*

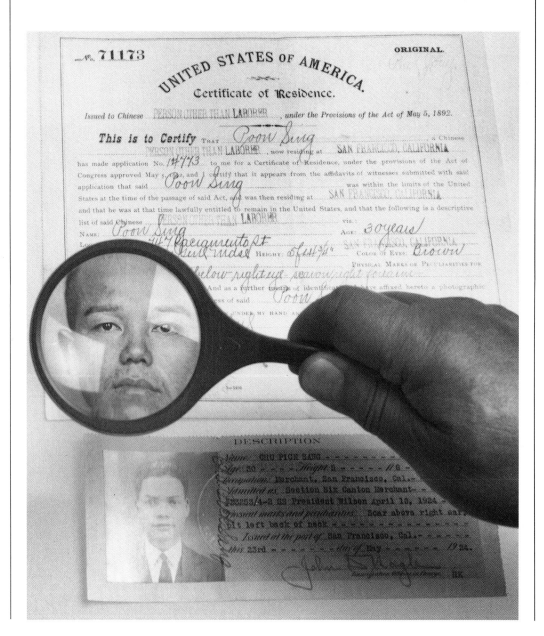

and allowed the United States to suspend Chinese immigration. Then in 1882, Congress passed the Chinese Exclusion Act, the first restrictive immigration legislation in American history aimed at a particular nationality or racial group. The act also prohibited the Chinese from seeking U.S. citizenship.

In 1892, Congress renewed the act, and in 1894, yet another U.S.-China treaty reaffirmed the exclusionary policy. In 1902, Congress enacted a permanent ban on Chinese immigration. The law even prohibited the return of Chinese immigrants who had left the United States for short periods of time. This ruling applied even to people who had left family and property behind in America.

**The Japanese.** By the 1880's, only a few hundred Japanese had come to the United States. These immigrants settled mainly in California and were generally well received. Most were unmarried men who established their own communities and maintained their traditional customs. With Chinese immigration at an end, the Japanese found work on railroads, farms, in the mines, and as domestic servants.

By 1900, about 25,000 Japanese immigrants had arrived in the United States. While many Japanese worked as farm laborers, often underbidding white workers for jobs, some Japanese managed to buy their own land and became successful farmers or truck gardeners, growing vegetables for sale. Before long, white workers and farmers in California resented the ambitious, resourceful, and clannish Japanese immigrants.

In 1906, the San Francisco Board of Education announced a plan to segregate all Asian students in separate schools. The scheme affected both Chinese and Japanese children, but only the Japanese government protested officially. President The-

*Led by Chinese American Paul Chow, the descendants of some immigrants are now working to have Angel Island restored. Said Chow, "Every group has its story. This is ours."*

odore Roosevelt, sensitive to Japan's newly established position as a world power and also very much aware of California's political strength, looked for a way out of the situation that would neither insult Japan nor ignore the anti-Asian sentiment on the West Coast. He found it in a "gentlemen's agreement."

Under the agreement, which was negotiated in 1907 and made effective the following year, Japan agreed to stop emigration of its workers to the United States. In return, the United States agreed that the school segregation order would be rescinded. The agreement did not please white San Franciscans who favored segregation, nor did it placate white Californians who wanted Japanese exclusion. It did, however, draw an international incident to a close before it became ugly.

## Other Restrictive Legislation.
In the meantime, anti-immigration sentiment, along with anti-Catholicism, grew throughout the nation as millions of newcomers arrived from central, southern, and eastern Europe. In response, Congress passed a patchwork of laws that restricted immigration.

An 1885 law banned the importation of *contract labor*— that is, workers for whom jobs had been arranged before they left home. However, household servants and skilled laborers were exempted. An 1891 law excluded several classes of people, including:

idiots, insane persons, paupers or persons likely to become a public charge, persons suffering from a loathsome or dangerous contagious disease,

---

## . . . Congress passed a patchwork of laws that restricted immigration.

---

However, there was a serious aftereffect. Until the action of the San Francisco school board, the Japanese people had looked on the United States as *Dai On Jin*, meaning *the Great Friendly People*. Now there was great resentment against America. Indignation ran so high, in fact, that a leading Japanese newspaper published an editorial that asked why Japan did not send warships to avenge the insult. Another immediate result was that Japan began spending a much higher percentage of its national budget on appropriations for its army and navy. A long-term result was that many of Japan's military leaders began to consider an eventual attack against the United States.

persons who have been convicted of a felony or other infamous crime or misdemeanor involving moral turpitude.

In 1903, Congress added prostitutes, epileptics, and professional beggars to the list. In 1901, an anarchist named Leon F. Czolgosz had assassinated President William McKinley. As a result, Congress also outlawed the entry of anarchists or anyone else who believed in the overthrow of governments by force.

## The American Protective Association.
By the early 1890's, nativists had added Roman Catholics to their list of

persons who should be restricted. Owing in great part to immigration, the number of American Roman Catholics had grown considerably over the years. Just as they had during the years of strong nativist sentiment before the Civil War, many Protestants again grew apprehensive that the Catholic Church aimed to undermine democracy, and they feared a papal plot to take over America. In addition, continual Catholic demands for government financial aid for the growing Catholic school system also disturbed Protestants. Many anti-Catholic people tended to overlook the fact that the Catholic schools had been started in part to counter the Protestant religious teachings often found in the public schools of the time. One such anti-Catholic group was the American Protective Association (APA).

The APA was the brainchild of Henry F. Bowers of Clinton, Iowa. Bowers, who detected Catholic conspiracy most everywhere, was a good friend of Clinton's mayor. When the mayor lost a reelection bid, Bowers blamed the defeat on the town's Irish Catholic millworkers who had voted as a bloc. The millworkers had indeed voted against Bowers' friend, because the mayor had alienated their union.

Over the next six years, Bowers traveled throughout the Middle West, crying out against the threat of Catholicism and drumming up membership. By 1894, APA membership

*Although some Americans wanted to restrict immigration, many others realized that the immigrants who came to the country as poor workers often soon added to the nation's wealth.*

Irving Berlin, a Russian Jew who came to the United States in the 1890's and authored the song "God Bless America" might not have ever entered the U.S. if the Immigration Restriction League had succeeded.

1890's, many Americans were convinced that immigrants from those regions were inferior, possibly dangerous to the nation's well-being, and would never fit well in America. A small band of New England intellectuals now took the lead in upholding Anglo-American culture and guarding the gates against the unrestricted influx of the so-called new immigration to the United States. In 1894, this group formed the Immigration Restriction League, with Prescott F. Hall, Robert DeCourcy Ward, and Charles Warren—all Harvard-educated Bostonians—as founders.

While the leaders of the Immigration Restriction League wanted to keep some groups of immigrants out of America, they also wished to avoid an obvious anti-immigration approach that might alienate the many Americans who did not share their Anglo-American ancestry. The League decided that a literacy test was the best way to accomplish its objective. Many recent immigrants were poor peasants who had never had a chance to learn to read and write. A literacy test would keep these immigrants out of the United States without making a politically hazardous exclusionary law.

In 1897, Congress passed a bill that required prospective immigrants to demonstrate the ability to read at least 40 words in any language, but President Grover Cleveland vetoed the legislation. Similar bills failed to get through Congress in 1898, 1902, and 1906. In 1913, a bill that did pass was promptly vetoed by President William Howard Taft.

lists had grown to include about 500,000 people.

The American Protective Association got legislation passed requiring that only the English language be used in parochial schools in both Illinois and Wisconsin. However, these laws were eventually declared unconstitutional, and the APA soon collapsed. Anti-Catholicism alone had proved to be too narrow a base on which to rally anti-immigrant sentiment.

## The Immigration Restriction League.

Although prejudice against immigrants from central, southern, and eastern Europe had religious aspects, it also had aspects that went beyond religion to other things. By the

## Eugenics and Immigration.

Having temporarily lost the battle for a literacy test, the Immigration Restriction League then turned to science for help. Opponents of restriction frequently argued that all immigrants could be transformed by the American environment they would encounter. Illiterates, for example, would learn to read and write once they entered the land of educational opportunity. However, the Immigration Restriction League dismissed such ideas as naive and scientifically insupportable. They drew on *eugenics*, the science of improving offspring through selective breeding, to support their beliefs. They contended that "racial" characteristics were fixed and could be changed only by mixing the different groups over several generations, a process they believed was more likely to degrade the "superior" than to elevate the "inferior." According to the league, American "racial purity" could be preserved only by excluding inferior types. Interestingly, the definition of race was not clear-cut. To some people, race was determined by skin color. Others believed religion, language group, or geographic region determined one's race. Today, many social scientists believe that the term *race* is not a valid one for grouping peoples.

Social scientists then took up eugenics and offered analyses presuming to show how all peoples could be categorized according to their hereditary types. They said that each type had its own traits that could not be changed by alterations in environment. Madison Grant provided the most influential arguments along those lines. In his *The Passing of the Great Race*, Grant contended that the fate of the "Nordic" peoples—meaning the northern and western Europeans he believed had made America great—was imperiled by the presence of groups from southern, central, and eastern Europe. Immigration restriction was no longer a matter of choice, according to eugenicists. Science demanded it.

*John Muir and Joseph Pulitzer both emigrated from Europe to the United States before the Civil War, but they made their most famous contributions to American life near the turn of the century. In 1892, Muir founded the Sierra Club, and in 1911, Pulitzer's will set in motion the founding of the Pulitzer Prizes.*

# PART 9: FROM WORLD WAR TO WORLD WAR

*The end of World War I brought an outpouring of joy across America, as shown in this painting called "Armistice Night."*

World War I ushered in a time of tumult and restriction for immigrants. In the early 1920's, there was a brief but powerful resurgence of the Ku Klux Klan, especially in the North and the Middle West. In the 1930's, overall immigration fell, though thousands of refugees fled to America from the dictatorial governments in Europe. Refugees continued to arrive after World War II ended in 1945.

The I.W.W. of the World Lead the STRI[KE] This means Succ[ess]

I am an American

CHINESE ▪ GERMAN ▪ CZECHO-SLOVAKIAN ▪ BRAZIL ▪ SPANISH ▪ JEWISH ▪ SCOTCH ▪ ROUMANIAN ▪ ENGLISH ▪ AUST[RIAN]

*The American social climate during the early 1900's was marked by strong emotions, expressed through such conflicting events as strikes, sometimes led by the I.W.W., and the staging of patriotic scenes like the one in this photograph of immigrant girls from 19 countries.*

# CHAPTER 26: PALMER, THE KLAN, AND DILLINGHAM

In the 1890's, Woodrow Wilson wrote that the immigrants from southern, central, and eastern Europe were:

multitudes of men of lowest class from the south of Italy, and men of the meaner sort out of Hungary and Poland, men out of the ranks where there was neither skill nor energy nor any initiative of quick intelligence; and they came in numbers which increased from year to year, as if the countries of the south of Europe were disburdening themselves of the more sordid and hapless elements of their population. . . . The Chinese were

ITALIAN ▪ POLISH ▪ RUSSIAN ▪ TURK ▪ GREEK ▪ IRISH ▪ LITHUNIAN ▪ PORTUGESE

more to be desired, as workmen if not as citizens, than most of the coarse crew that came crowding in every year at the eastern ports.

Wilson's opponents in the presidential campaign of 1912 used those remarks against him, and he lost a great percentage of the immigrant vote. As a result and perhaps somewhat hypocritically, Wilson as President adopted a different point of view on immigration. In 1915, he vetoed

an immigration bill that contained a literacy test on the grounds that it:

embodies a radical departure from the tradition and long established policy of this country. . . . It seeks to close all but entirely the gates of asylum which have always been open to those who could find [it] nowhere else . . . and it excludes those to whom the opportunities of elementary education have been denied

*One immigrant of the era was an Italian nun, Saint Frances Xavier Cabrini, who came to America in 1889 and became a citizen in 1909. She founded hospitals, orphanages, schools, and free clinics in her adopted homeland.*

without regard to their character, their purpose or their natural ability.

After his reelection in 1916, Wilson vetoed another exclusionary law. This time, however, Congress overrode the veto, and in 1917, a literacy test became one of America's immigration requirements.

The Literacy Test. The literacy test applied only to immigrants over the age of 16, and it required the reading of a maximum of 40 words in any language. Family members over age 55 were admitted to the country whether they could read or not, provided one other family member had passed the literacy test. Political refugees and people fleeing from religious persecution were exempt from the literacy test, as were immigrants from Mexico and Canada.

Once a literacy test became law, would-be immigrants sensibly prepared for it. If necessary, they memorized short passages from printed material, and indeed, most newcomers passed the test. Of about 1.3 million immigrants who came to the United States between 1918 and 1921, only 6,142, or 0.4 per cent, were rejected because of an inability to read.

The War and Things Germanic. On April 2, 1917, President Wilson asked Congress for a declaration of war against Germany, and America entered World War I. As patriotic fervor increased, a number of things Germanic vanished or underwent name changes in the United States. Bismarck herring and many other German foods disappeared from restaurants. Sauerkraut survived under the name of Liberty cabbage, as did hamburgers, but now they were known as Salisbury steaks. German shepherd dogs became Alsatian shepherds, and dachshunds lost popularity as pets. Musical groups rarely performed the works of Wagner, Beethoven, or Schubert.

The legislatures in Montana, Delaware, Iowa, and other states passed laws prohibiting the teaching of the German language. Boy Scouts in many cities burned some German-language newspapers in the streets, and some such papers ceased publication. The windows of German-owned shops were smashed, and companies, communities, and people with German names had them legally changed.

Members of the Industrial Workers of the World, a labor organization whose members were known as *Wobblies*, spoke out against the war, as did some socialists. They insisted that its only beneficiaries would be capitalists who had long manipulated and oppressed workers. In the public eye, the Wobblies became connected with pro-Germanism, and the group fared badly during the war. In 1917, the Wobblies organized strikes by copper miners in the Southwest and by migrant lumberjacks in the Northwest. Both strikes led to violence. Armed vigilantes rounded up Wobblies—real or suspected—in New Mexico

*During World War I, German immigrants came under suspicion as possible spies and saboteurs. In New York City, officials fingerprinted them to have records in case they were accused later of any crimes.*

and Arizona, and the Department of Justice raided the meeting halls of the Wobblies in several cities. More than 300 Wobblies were tried for violating the Espionage Act.

The I.W.W. was also responsible for some of the American labor movement's most popular songs, many of which were parodies of revival hymns. Among them was "The Preacher and the Slave," which included a line about *pie in the sky*. Ever since, Americans have used the term *pie in the sky* to refer to something promised in the future that will probably never come to pass.

The writer of "The Preacher and the Slave" was a Swedish-born dockworker and I.W.W. organizer named Joe Hill. In 1915, he was tried in Salt Lake City, Utah, and convicted of murder despite the lack of hard evidence. The night before he was to be executed by a firing squad, Hill sent the following telegram to the head of the I.W.W.: "Don't waste any time in

mourning. Organize." Some 30,000 people attended Hill's funeral in Chicago. On the following May Day—an international labor holiday—supporters scattered Hill's ashes in every state in the nation except Utah, as well as in many countries around the world.

The Drive for Americanization. After the United States entered World War I, pressure developed to create national solidarity through "One Hundred Per Cent Americanization." The Ford Motor Company, for example, ran an English-language school and required all immigrant employees to attend before and after work two days per week. The U.S. Congress aided the Americanization drive by passing a revenue act in 1918 that taxed the incomes of "nonresident" aliens at a rate twice as high as the tax rate for U.S. citizens and "res-

*At the Ford Motor Company, graduates of its English school declare their patriotism in a group photo. Ford employees trained in "Americanization" served as teachers for the school.*

This 1919 cartoon symbolized the Red scare in America. It depicts a bearded Russian Bolshevik revolutionary creeping out from under an American flag.

tice Oliver Wendell Holmes, and financier J. Pierpont Morgan. The people who mailed the bombs were never caught, but many people believed that the bombs were sent by immigrants and Communists.

# The Big Red Roundup.

In May 1919, a bomb exploded outside the Washington, D.C., home of A. Mitchell Palmer, the newly appointed attorney general of the United States. Palmer, who had presidential ambitions, thought he saw a chance for some positive publicity. He declared "war" on terrorists and left-wingers of all kinds, and he said he planned to sweep America clean of such troublesome and dangerous foreign elements.

In September, 376,000 steelworkers went on strike for better working conditions and higher wages. Numerous workers in other industries also went on strike about this time. Many other Americans believed that radicals had fomented these strikes. As a result, Palmer gained strong public support.

On Nov. 7, 1919—the second anniversary of the Russian Revolution—Palmer's agents in a dozen cities raided meeting places that were frequented by workers of Russian ancestry. Palmer's men seized people without warrants and jailed them without cause—some 650 were jailed in New York City alone. In December, about 250 people were deported to Russia. Most were guilty of nothing more than having declared themselves to be *anarchists*, radicals who believe that all forms of government should be abolished, which in itself was not a crime. During the first six weeks of 1920, federal agents and local police indiscriminately seized about 6,000 people in 33 cities, mostly without warrants.

Palmer was widely praised in newspaper editorials for his roundups of "Red aliens." However, as peace

ident" aliens. The National Americanization Committee turned annual Fourth of July celebrations into "National Americanization Day" under the slogan "Many Peoples, But One Nation." Hundreds of churches, schools, fraternal groups, women's clubs, civic organizations, patriotic societies, and philanthropies also embraced the goals of the "One Hundred Per Cent" program.

Germany's defeat and the end of World War I led to a decline in anti-German feelings in America, but fears of another kind soon arose. These fears concerned a different kind of foreign influence—Communism. Although the two Communist Parties in the United States had fewer than 75,000 members in all, the general public became convinced, in part because elected officials said so, that these "Reds" posed a real danger to America. This was especially true in 1919, when mail bombs were sent to prominent Americans such as John D. Rockefeller, Supreme Court Jus-

returned to the labor front—with employers being the winners in most cases—the general public lost interest in the Red menace. At the same time, people and organizations with a strong regard for civil liberties and the due process of law began to assert themselves. Palmer tried—but failed—to have 3,500 of the "Red aliens" deported, and then, in what seemed like a desperate move, he overstepped himself.

In April 1920, Palmer announced that bombs would explode on May Day—May 1—in cities across the country. Police forces and federal troops were placed on alert, and state militias were called out. However, May Day came and went—peacefully. Discredited, Palmer became a national laughingstock, his presidential ambitions in ruins.

One result of the Palmer raids was the formation in 1920 of the American Civil Liberties Union (ACLU). Its purpose was to protect the rights set forth in the U.S. Constitution. Throughout the years, the ACLU has played a role in every major civil liberties case that has moved through the U.S. court system.

This involvement includes the Sacco-Vanzetti case of the early 1920's, in which two Italian immigrants who were anarchists were convicted of a

On Dec. 21, 1919, the New York Times newspaper published this cartoon showing Uncle Sam sending a group of Russian revolutionaries back to "Messrs. Lenin & Trotsky—Russia." The cartoon's caption said, "The Cheerful Giver—Or, Do Your Christmas Shipping Early." In fact, one self-avowed Russian anarchist in America, Emma Goldman, was deported that year. She had come to the United States in 1885.

*In many instances, Klan membership became a "family affair," and there were a variety of ceremonies in which to participate. In 1927, this couple had their seven-month-old son inducted into the Klan.*

Massachusetts murder on circumstantial evidence. Most historians believe that Sacco and Vanzetti were convicted because of the national hysteria about immigrants and the Red Scare. The men were executed in 1927.

# Nativism Revisited—the Ku Klux Klan.

The great surge toward industrialization that had begun with the Civil War brought young people from rural areas, along with immigrants, to urban areas where the jobs were. Those who remained on the farms and in the small towns of America viewed the nation's growing cities with mixed emotions—awe, apprehension, and even fear.

To many rural people, city life appeared to be unnatural, unhealthy, immoral, and dangerous to the traditional American values of religion, family, and community. Hoping to reinforce those values, hundreds of thousands of rural people joined an organization that promised to uphold these beliefs. At the same time, this group fueled the fears of many people about the ideas and institutions they considered to be un-American. The organization was the infamous Ku Klux Klan.

The original Klansmen had organized during the Reconstruction era in the 1870's to terrorize African Americans. More than 40 years later, on Oct. 15, 1915, by the light of a burning cross on Stone Mountain, Ga., the sons and grandsons of those earlier Klan members revived the Ku Klux Klan as a fraternal and "patriotic" group that not only retained its original anti-black beliefs but also added Jews, immigrants, and Roman Catholics to its list of "enemies of America."

By 1920, the Klan had only about 5,000 members, mostly in the South. Then in the summer of 1921, the head of the Klan contracted with two highly skilled publicity agents to conduct membership drives in exchange for $8 out of every $10 in initiation fees they collected. Their very high-pressure sales tactics soon spread the Klan into the Southwest and the Middle West and increased membership to more than 1 million.

circuses, carnivals, and fireworks displays. There was also, however, a more sinister aspect to the Klan.

Klan Targets. The Klan, like other anti-Semitic groups, labeled all Jews as international conspirators who were bent on destroying capitalism and the American way of life. On the other hand, Jews supposedly controlled a banking group that planned to take over the world by financial manipulation of the economy. Jews also were said to spread subversive ideas across America through their involvement in the movie industry.

Roman Catholics were another Klan target. Once again, Catholics

---

## Unlike the secret societies of the 1800's, the Klan produced no political party of its own.

---

The Klan attracted people who had become confused, bewildered, and angry about the rapid social changes occurring in America and longed to return to a mythic time of order and tranquility that they believed existed in the past. Hirman Wesley Evans, a Klan leader, or Imperial Wizard, said:

> We demand a return of power into the hands of the everyday, not highly cultured, not overly intellectualized but entirely unspoiled and not de-Americanized average citizens of the old stock.

Membership in the Klan gave many people a feeling of belonging, and in some respects, Klan chapters behaved much like most fraternal or civic-minded organizations. Local chapters sponsored community dinners, square dances, athletic contests,

were accused of putting loyalty to the pope above loyalty to the nation. The Klan condemned parochial schools and lobbied for state laws that required daily Bible reading in elementary classrooms — from the Protestant version of the text.

Klan members also favored strict curbs on immigration. They said that Jews, Catholics, and millions of other people from central, southern, and eastern Europe were inferior peoples who would "mongrelize" the "American race" and were responsible for most of the nation's social problems.

The Klan and Politics. Unlike the secret societies of the 1800's, the Klan produced no political party of its own. Nevertheless, the organization achieved considerable political influ-

*Crusading editor William Allen White made his small-town Kansas newspaper into one of the most famous papers in the world. For more than four decades, White's editorials played an important part in the political affairs of the United States, and he won the 1923 Pulitzer Prize for editorial writing. Thus, his defeat for the Kansas governorship through the efforts of the Klan shocked many in the nation.*

ence. In many areas, candidates for public office could not win without Klan support, and Klan opposition was the political kiss of death.

Although much of the Klan's political success was on the local level, Klan voters in Oklahoma helped elect a governor and a U.S. senator who were sympathetic to their causes. In Kansas, Klan opposition to William Allen White, the nationally known editor of the *Emporia Gazette*—and one of the few public figures to denounce the Klan—helped defeat White in his bid for the Kansas governor's office in 1924.

That same year, the Klan—also with considerable success—displayed its political muscle at the Democratic national convention. Klan supporters kept the convention deadlocked until a lackluster candidate named John W. Davis was finally nominated for President. Later, Davis was easily defeated by Calvin Coolidge.

**The Klan's Downfall.** Finally, the Klan's strength began to fade. In Louisiana, for example, an anti-Klan governor got a law passed that required all Klansmen to give up the traditional white hoods that they used to mask their faces in large demonstrations. Oklahoma, New York, Michigan, Iowa, and Minnesota also passed similar legislation. In Chicago—which had about 1 million Roman Catholic residents—the City Council passed anti-Klan resolutions. The newly formed American Unity League broke the secrecy seal on Klan membership by publishing the names of Klan members. The league urged boycotts of businesses operated by Klan members, and it also organized anti-Klan rallies.

The Klan's real downfall began in Indiana, where the Klan had gained a major influence over state government and 200,000 people had re-

*In the 1920's, Klansmen became so bold that they even wore their hoods in public and posed for pictures, as they did here in 1921. Black leader Marcus Garvey, a Jamaican immigrant, tried to instill in African Americans a sense of racial pride, which the Klan and others tried to strip away. By the 1920's, Garvey's Universal Negro Improvement Association had 2 million members in 38 states.*

cently gathered in Kokomo at the largest Klan meeting in history. David C. Stephenson, a membership salesman who was credited with signing up about 250,000 recruits at $10 a head, became the state's Klan leader. Even as rumors spread about his sexual and alcoholic escapades, Stephenson lived lavishly on a grand estate in Indianapolis and cruised aboard his large yacht.

In 1925, the lid blew off Stephenson's world—and that of the Klan in general—when he was accused of transporting a woman across state lines for immoral purposes and of contributing to her death by suicide. Stephenson was convicted of second-degree murder and sentenced to a long prison term, largely on the basis of the woman's own testimony, which had been recorded before she died.

Many Klan members now began to wonder how *their* initiation fees and dues had been used. Law enforcement agencies in several states started investigating Klan leaders, uncovering fraud and other corruption in more than one case. The Klan now became fair game almost everywhere.

# Getting Back at the Klan.

Groups of former Klan victims now rallied together to hound and harass Klan members, sometimes using the Klan's own illegal methods in the process. For example, a bomb destroyed the office of the Klan newspaper in Chicago. In suburban Pittsburgh, a mob attacked a Klan parade with stones and bottles, killing one Klansman and injuring several others. In Steubenville, Ohio, 3,000 people raided a Klan meeting of only 100 members, and in Perth Amboy, N.J., a group of Roman Catholics and Jews led a mob of 6,000 against a Klan meeting. They took on the entire city police and fire departments in order to stone, beat, and kick about 500 Klan members.

Finally, the nation seemed to reach some degree of peace with itself. Although the Klan continued to be troublesome, it was only a ghost of the robust and politically powerful group it had been in the early 1920's.

# The Dillingham Commission.

The Ku Klux Klan had supported immigration restriction, and Congress passed a severely restrictive law in 1924, the year Klan membership reached its peak. That law had been preceded by temporary legislation in 1921, and by much study and discussion over several years.

Starting in 1907, the government-sponsored Dillingham Commission made a study of every conceivable aspect of immigration. More than three years later, the commission published 41 volumes of data, much of it about the economic aspects of immigration. In its works, the commission grouped immigrants into two categories—"old immigrants" and "new immigrants." According to the commission, the old immigrants, who came from western and northern Europe, had represented a movement of families, and its non-English-speaking members merged into the dominant Anglo-American culture without great difficulty. Many of the old immigrants became farmers, the commission said.

In the 1880's, large numbers of new immigrants had begun to arrive from eastern, central, and southern Europe. The commission concluded that the new immigrants consisted largely of unskilled men who planned to earn money and then return to their homeland, and who congregated in industrial areas where they kept up their traditional cultures and resisted assimilation. Actually, the only thing new about the new immigrants was that they came from different geographic areas than their predecessors. Their reasons for coming and their experiences, though, were much the same as those of immigrants in earlier times.

# New and Old Compared.

Men had always made up the great majority of the first immigrant groups from any new area. Women and children usually followed once the male immigrants became established. The so-called new immigrants also were hardly the first to set up their own communities and keep alive the language and traditional ways of their homeland. The Germans, Norwegians, and Swedes had all done that, too.

> ## Although the new immigrants came from different countries, they behaved much like the groups that had preceded them.

It was true that immigrant peasants from central, southern, and eastern Europe usually did not become farmers in America, but there were at least two good reasons for this. By the time they arrived, the best—and especially the low-priced—land had been taken. In addition, most immigrants could not afford the investment in machinery, buildings, and fencing that competitive American agriculture required by that time.

Most of the new immigrants were unskilled, but so were many members of the earlier groups—the Irish, for example. The recent arrivals tended to congregate in New York City, Pittsburgh, Chicago, and other large cities because that was where the most jobs for unskilled workers were. They lived together in slums because no other housing was available to them, as had been true for almost all other, earlier immigrant groups.

Not until the late 1800's did Russia, Austria-Hungary, Turkey, and Italy allow their people to leave freely. At about that same time, steamship lines expanded their routes to include ports on the Mediterranean Sea and the Black Sea..

The relatively cheap steamship fares and the short, safe transatlantic passage also encouraged many immigrants to return home once they had accumulated nest eggs in America. They could go back to the old country with much better chances for an improved life, thanks to money they had earned and saved in the United States.

Altogether, more people from the central, southern, and eastern regions of Europe returned to their homeland than did people from the western and northern regions. When broken down by national origins, however, the picture was quite different. While the return rate for Italians was high, it was also high among the English, Germans, and Scandinavians. It was low among the Jews, Armenians, and Portuguese.

Beginning in the 1890's, immigration from northern and western Europe slowed down. The birth rate in those regions had been declining, and in addition, rapid industrialization in Germany and the Scandinavian countries after 1890 created more jobs at home.

Although the new immigrants came from different countries, they behaved much like the groups that had preceded them. However, the American general public, with a fair amount of encouragement from their elected officials, still tended to deplore the arrival of so many newcomers from eastern, southern, and central Europe. For a while at least, these latest immigrants suffered under the same yoke of prejudice as the newcomers of earlier days.

*The 1920 ratification of the 19th Amendment to the Constitution gave women in the United States—both native-born and naturalized citizens—the right to vote.*

Over the years, quite a few American writers, artists, and performers chose to leave the United States and live abroad. Known as expatriates, some of these talented people lived outside in New York City in 1843, James left America when he was in his early 30's. He lived first in Paris and then in London, becoming a British citizen in 1915, the year before his death.

# EXPATRIATES

the United States for only a few years. Others spent most of their lives abroad.

Novelist Henry James was one of America's earliest and most noteworthy expatriates. Born Also born in the 1840's was American painter Mary Cassatt. Originally from Pennsylvania, Cassatt spent most of her life in France. An impressionist painter, Cas-

satt was greatly influenced by her French contemporaries, especially Manet and Degas, whose friendship and esteem she enjoyed.

America of the 1920's produced a whole group of artistic expatriates, most of whom chose to live in Paris. Many of these people had been disillusioned by World War I. They were also reacting against the anti-intellectualism and racial prejudice that characterized Americans of that era.

Dancer Josephine Baker was one example. Born in a St. Louis, Mo., slum in 1906, she was dancing in the chorus line of an all-black musical review by the time she was a teenager. By 1925, she was a featured player in musical revues in Paris. Soon she achieved stardom as a dancer and a blues singer in the Folies Bergere. In 1937, she became a French citizen. So lasting was her popularity that when she died in 1975, some 20,000 people attended her funeral in Paris.

Americans living in France or elsewhere in Europe during the 1920's eventually made up

**Josephine Baker became a star in Paris.**

a who's who of American artists and people of letters. The list included John Dos Passos, e. e. cummings, and F. Scott Fitzgerald, whose 1934 work, *Tender Is the Night*, describes the troubled lives of a wealthy American expatriate couple in Europe after World War I. Other expatriate writers included Archibald MacLeish, Ernest Hemingway, and Sherwood Anderson. Years later, Hemingway wrote a book about his life in Paris. Called *A Moveable Feast*, it was an instant best-

**Mary Cassatt was a friend of French impressionist Edgar Degas, who painted this picture of her.**

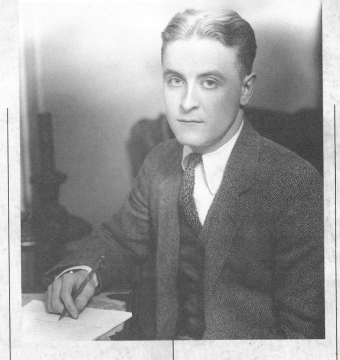

F. Scott Fitzgerald quickly became famous after his first book, *This Side of Paradise,* was published in 1920.

the Johns Hopkins School of Medicine in Baltimore. Opting for a literary life, Stein settled in Paris in 1903 with her brother Leo, an

The stock market crash of 1929 and the rise of dictatorships in Europe led to many changes. Gertrude Stein and a few others remained in France. Hemingway went to Spain, where civil war began in 1936. Others returned to America. Fitzgerald,

seller in the United States.

The guiding light around which many of these expatriates gathered was Gertrude Stein. On Saturday evenings, she presided over a weekly salon in her

apartment at 27 Rue de Flaurus.

Herself an expatriate, Stein was born in Allegheny, Penn., in 1874. She graduated from Radcliffe College and then studied medicine for a time at

This photo of Ernest Hemingway was taken in Paris in 1923.

art critic and collector. Stein published several works of her own, but she became especially well known for the counsel and encouragement she offered painters, writers, musicians, and others of an artistic bent.

for example, settled in Hollywood, Calif., where he wrote screenplays for the movie industry. An era of artistic flowering was ending. World War II soon loomed for people everywhere.

Pablo Picasso painted this portrait of Gertrude Stein in the fall of 1906.

The equations on the blackboard:

$$\alpha = \frac{\hbar^2}{ec}$$

$$= K.E.$$

$$c^4 + c^2 p^2 = E$$

*Despite the Great Depression of the 1930's, many immigrants still came to America. Two who arrived in 1938 were Italian physicist Enrico Fermi—a Nobel Prize winner—and German architect Ludwig Mies van der Rohe.*

# CHAPTER 27: REFUGEES, RESTRICTIONS, AND RACIAL PREJUDICE

World War I had ended with dire predictions of a huge wave of immigrants to the United States. Between 1918 and 1921, more than 1 million immigrants arrived from Europe, but the numbers were not nearly as large as had been anticipated.

Nevertheless, labor unions and organizations such as the Immigration Restriction League continued to press for restriction, in some cases demanding a

*In 1942, the history of American immigration entered one of its darkest periods: the forced internment of Japanese Americans. Tens of thousands of U.S. citizens spent years in camps such as the one at Manzanar, Calif., shown here in a photograph by Ansel Adams. In May 1942, photographer Dorothea Lange took the above picture of a grandfather and his grandchildren waiting for evacuation from Hayward, Calif., to one of the camps.*

two-year moratorium on all immigration. As economic recovery began in the early 1920's, business and industry tended to oppose immigration restriction since they saw immigrants as a source of inexpensive labor. As industries installed more labor-saving machinery, however, the interest in cheap labor diminished somewhat, and so did the industrialists' opposition to restriction.

In Congress, the level of enthusiasm for reducing the flow of immigrants tended to reflect the number of immigrants in a Congress member's district. However, enough legislators favored restriction for Congress to dust off the Dillingham Report in search of ideas and ammunition to use in the writing of new immigration legislation. Dillingham, who was still in the Senate, suggested a quota plan for admission that would be based on the number of foreign-born people of each nationality that were counted in the U.S. census of 1910. Dillingham's plan became the basis for the Quota Act of 1921.

Under that act, 3 per cent of the number of people of each nationality represented in the 1910 census would be admitted, with the ceiling placed at a total of 358,000 immigrants per year. The plan would allow about 200,000 immigrants from northern and western Europe, and about 155,000 immigrants from the remainder of the continent. The law allowed for many exemptions, so the total number of actual immigrants in any one year could turn out to be twice the number admitted under the quota system. The 1921 legislation was meant to be a temporary measure until a permanent arrangement could be worked out. That did not happen

In addition, Congress drew up the National Origins Act, which would go into effect in 1929. Then, aside from exemptions, total immigration would be reduced to about 153,700 people per year. In addition, the proportions of national representation were frozen at the levels indicated by the 1920 census. This allowed five times as many immigrants from northern and western Europe as from other European countries. The National Origins Act excluded Japanese, Chinese, and other Asians from citizenship—and hence from entry—and required that all would-be immigrants obtain visas from American consulates abroad, thus providing a preliminary screening of all potential entries. No longer would the admis-

# Economic depression did more to dampen immigration to the United States than any restrictive law was able to accomplish.

immediately, and in 1922, the Quota Act was extended to 1924.

In 1921 and 1922, the immigrant quotas for western and northern Europe were not filled. However, there were far more potential immigrants from southern, central, and eastern Europe than the law allowed.

Despite the restrictions, the number of immigrants from southern, central, and eastern Europe was still too large to satisfy those people who wanted assurance that the Anglo-American culture would remain dominant in the United States. Consequently, in 1924, the National Origins Act changed the quota year to 1890 and the ratio of immigrants to 2 per cent of each nationality, thus giving an even larger percentage to northern and western Europeans.

sion decision be made solely at reception centers such as Ellis Island. Thus ended an era in American immigration history that stretched back across more than three centuries. The Golden Door was still ajar, but just barely.

An unexpected result of these immigration restrictions was that many middle- and upper-class Americans found themselves largely without domestic servants. No longer were immigrants available to work as butlers, cooks, housekeepers, laundresses, and maids. As a result, people were forced to develop substitutes for hired help. The number of restaurants, laundries, and carpet-cleaning firms increased. Labor-saving devices for the home—such as electric refrigerators, electric irons, modern electric ranges, and washing machines—be-

On Oct. 1, 1940, Albert Einstein took the oath of American citizenship at a ceremony in Trenton, N.J. On his right is his secretary, Helene Dukas, and on his left is his daughter Margot.

came popular. Packaged, precooked, and frozen foods were developed. Cocktail parties replaced dinner parties as a way of entertaining large numbers of people at home.

**I**mmigration in the 1930's. Economic depression did more to dampen immigration to the United States than any restrictive law was able to accomplish. With American unemployment at about 13 million people by 1933, there were no jobs for long-time residents, to say nothing of immigrants. In 1931, only 97,129 immigrants came to America, and the annual total stayed below 100,000 per year throughout the decade. The low point was 1933, when only 23,068 immigrants made the journey.

Thousands of those who came to America in the 1930's were refugees, many of them fleeing the anti-Semitic and anti-intellectual regimes that arose in Germany and elsewhere. In Germany, Adolf Hitler's Nazis had ruthlessly purged the universities and scientific institutions of their best people in many fields. Without jobs or good prospects for the future, many of these people decided to emigrate to the United States and elsewhere in the Western Hemisphere. However, these immigrants were much different from the unskilled and illiterate masses that had characterized the immigrant groups of the past. These latest immigrants were often middle-aged and middle-class, and some of them were even world-famous.

Certainly the most famous of all was Albert Einstein, a Jew. In 1905, Einstein had written three papers concerning various aspects of physics, and in 1921, he had received the Nobel Prize for this work. In 1933, while

*Architect I.M. Pei, right, came to America from China in 1935. Among his many well-known designs are those for the John F. Kennedy Library in Boston, Mass., and the addition to the Louvre museum in Paris, France.*

*German-born painter Josef Albers, below, also came to the United States in the 1930's. He later taught at Black Mountain College and at Yale University.*

he was visiting the United States, the Nazis stripped him of his German citizenship, his academic and intellectual positions, and his property in Germany. As luck would have it, however, Princeton University had already invited Einstein to become a member of the staff at its newly created Institute for Advanced Study. Einstein accepted the offer and settled down in Princeton, N.J. In 1940, he became a U.S. citizen.

Other Jewish refugees, however, were not as fortunate as Einstein. In 1939, the ocean liner *St. Louis* left Germany for Havana, Cuba. It was carrying 930 Jews, of whom 734 were bound for the United States. They had fulfilled American immigration requirements and held quota numbers entitling them to enter the United States from three months to three years after they reached Cuba. Before they arrived, however, the Cuban government changed its immigration laws. The temporary visas the refugees held were worthless.

After several days of frantic negotiations, the *St. Louis* was forced to leave Havana. But its captain—reluctant to return to Germany—set

sail for the United States. For a while, the ship hovered within sight of Miami, Fla., shadowed by a U.S. Coast Guard boat with instructions to prevent any refugees from jumping ship and swimming ashore. Telegrams to President Roosevelt from the ship's passengers, begging for asylum, went unanswered.

Finally, the *St. Louis* returned to Europe. Several nations—Belgium, France, Great Britain, and the Netherlands—agreed to admit the refugees. Less than three months later, however, World War II broke out, and almost all the Jews who had been turned away from the United States died in Nazi concentration camps.

Other famous immigrant physicists included Leo Szilard, Edward Teller, and Eugene P. Wigner—all from Hungary—and Enrico Fermi from Italy. During World War II, these men proved instrumental in helping America develop the world's first atomic bomb.

Refugee artists during this time included Marcel Duchamp. Among the composers and conductors were Béla Bartók, Arnold Schoenberg, Igor Stravinsky, and Bruno Walter. There were also architects, such as Ludwig Mies van der Rohe and Walter

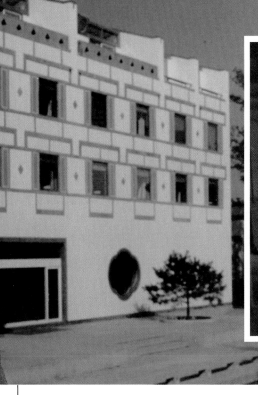

Polish-born pianist Arthur Rubinstein came to America in 1939 and became a U.S. citizen in 1946.

Gropius, and many leading writers. Social scientists included Hannah Arendt, Paul Lazarsfeld, Kurt Lewin, Herbert Marcuse, and Leo Strauss. Erich Fromm, Erik Erikson, and Helene Deutsch represented the field of psychoanalysis.

Such well-known individuals usually had little trouble continuing their work in America. Many middle-class refugees, such as bankers, physicians, dentists, engineers, business people, lawyers, and lesser-known scientists had a more difficult time. Often, they had to accept work as dishwashers, elevator operators, night watchmen, or hospital orderlies. Most, however, eventually found employment in the fields for which they had been trained.

Some refugees got help in immigrating and settling from various voluntary organizations. Many of the Jewish immigrants were aided by the Jewish Labor Committee, the American Jewish Council, and the Anti-Defamation League of B'nai B'rith. These immigrants were the luckier ones. Neither Congress nor the U.S. Department of State proved willing to loosen immigration restrictions to favor the political refugees of the 1930's. Many more would have

gained entry and their lives would have been saved if these restrictions had been lifted.

# Hollywood.

The 1930's also saw the rise to movie stardom of a number of immigrants, most of whom were from Europe. One such immigrant was English-born Cary Grant, who achieved his first major success in a 1933 film called *She Done Him Wrong*. Throughout the rest of the 1930's, Grant continued to star in witty comedies such as *Bringing Up Baby* and *The Philadelphia Story*. In the 1940's and 1950's, Grant starred in several thrillers, such as *To Catch a Thief* and *North by Northwest*, both of which were directed by Alfred Hitchcock, another English immigrant. In 1942, Grant became a U.S. citizen.

Alfred Hitchcock came from England to the United States in 1939, when he was already a successful film director. His first American movie, *Rebecca*, won the Academy Award for best picture in 1940. Hitchcock's later American movies included *Spellbound*, *The Birds*, and the scary *Psycho*. From 1955 to 1965, Hitchcock produced and hosted a weekly television show in which he frequently made wry, eerie jokes to entice the viewers.

almost five decades later. Among her most famous films are *Queen Christina*, *Anna Karenina*, and *Ninotchka*.

Other foreign-born actresses and actors who came to Hollywood in the 1930's included Vivian Leigh and Leslie Howard, both of whom starred in *Gone with the Wind*. Misha Auer, a Russian immigrant, played in well-known comedies such as *My Man Godfrey* and *You Can't Take It with You*. English actor Eric Blore found a "home" in the 1930's movies that starred dancers Ginger Rogers and Fred Astaire. In various films with them, Blore played a butler, a waiter, and a fake minister.

One of the most famous actresses of all times, Swedish-born Greta Garbo came to the United States in 1925 and pursued her movie career in Hollywood until her unexpected retirement in 1941 at the height of her fame. She lived an intensely private life in New York City until her death

**Japanese Internment.** After Japan's surprise attack on Pearl Harbor, Ha., on Dec. 7, 1941, the United States entered World War II and again faced the question of immigrant loyalty. Although it was not supported by the facts, there was a widely held belief—supported by a statement by the secretary of the Navy—that the Pearl Harbor attack had been aided by sabotage and undercover activity by Japanese immigrants and Japanese Americans in Hawaii. Soon, too, the armies of Japan made several startling advances elsewhere. On Dec. 10, Guam fell. On Dec. 24, Japan captured Wake Island, and on Dec. 25, it occupied Hong Kong. On Dec. 27, Manila was evacuated by the American army, and they retreated to the Bataan Peninsula, where they were forced to surrender unconditionally the following April.

On Feb. 14, 1942, Lieutenant General John L. De Witt, the commanding general of the Western Defense Command, which included the western United States, but not Hawaii, wrote to the secretary of war that:

> In the war in which we are now engaged racial affinities are not severed by migration. The Japanese race is an enemy race and while many second and third generation Japanese born on United States soil, possessed of United States citizenship, have become "Americanized," the racial strains are undiluted. . . . [There] is no ground for assuming that any Japanese, barred from assimilation by convention as he is, though born and raised in the United States, will not turn against the nation when the final test of loyalty comes. It, therefore, follows that along the vital Pacific Coast over 112,000 potential enemies, of Japanese extraction, are at large today. . . . The very fact that no sabotage has taken place to date is a disturbing and confirming indication that such action will be taken.

On Feb. 19, 1942, President Franklin Roosevelt issued the executive order that led to the *internment*, or forced confinement, of about 110,000 people for several years. The order prohibited all Americans of Japanese descent from living, working, or traveling on the West Coast of the United States, where almost all Japanese Americans in the continental United States lived at the time. These Japanese Americans were moved to

*Evacuees to the internment camps could take only the amount of baggage they could carry, which often required much anguished sorting of a lifetime's possessions.*

bleak barrack camps, mostly in desolate areas of the West.

For many decades, Japanese immigrants had been barred by law from becoming naturalized American citizens. However, their children and grandchildren were American citizens by birth. Thus, about 65 per cent of the people sent to the camps were second- and third-generation Americans. Most of these people lived in California, where they made up 1.6 per cent of the population in the 1940 census. Interestingly, in Hawaii—the site of actual bombing by Japan—people of Japanese ancestry made up more than one-third of the population. However, no general internment occurred there.

The evacuation to the camps began on March 31, 1942. Once a notice of evacuation was posted, a representative of each family went to a control center where the family was registered, assigned a number, told what they could take with them, and instructed when and where to report. Many years later, one person wrote:

> Henry went to the Control Station to register the family. He came home with twenty tags, all numbered 10710, tags to be attached to each piece of baggage, and one to hang from our coat lapels. From then on, we were known as Family #10710.

About the trip itself, one woman recalled:

> On May 16, 1942, at 9:30 a.m., we departed . . . for an unknown destination. To this day, I can remember vividly the plight of the elderly, some on stretchers, orphans herded onto the train by caretakers, and especially a young couple with 4 pre-school children. The mother had two frightened toddlers hanging on to her coat. In her arms, she carried two crying babies. The father had diapers and other baby paraphernalia strapped to his back. In his hands he struggled with duffle bag and suitcase. The shades were drawn on the train for our entire trip. Military police patrolled the aisles.

Finally in December 1944, the exclusion order was lifted, and Japanese Americans were allowed to return to the West Coast.

In the meantime, an army battalion composed entirely of Japanese Americans—many coming directly from the relocation camps—had earned 900 Purple Hearts in battle in North Africa and Italy. This famous 100th Battalion, along with the much-decorated 442nd Regimental Combat Team, which suffered 9,486 casualties during the war, helped show other Americans that the loyalty of Japanese Americans should not lightly be questioned.

*By September 1942, there were 16 assembly centers, including this one, Tanforan, where more than 7,800 people lived. As elsewhere, each family lived in a single tar-papered barrack room, regardless of the number of people in the family.*

Despite their freedom, though, many Japanese Americans had little to return to, since many of them had lost their life savings in the process. As one woman later said about her father who had owned one of the largest nurseries in southern California:

He had 20 acres of choice land on Wilshire and Sepulveda. He had very choice customers [such] as Will Rogers and Shirley Temple's parents. . . . But wealth and standing did not save my father from being arrested. . . . When . . . [order] 9066 mandated that all Japanese were to evacuate . . . and my mother on her own without father, father taken to Missoula, was not able to consult him. . . . So what did she do but she gave all of the nursery stock to the U.S. Government, the Veterans Hospital which was adjoining the nursery. It was written up in the local newspaper along with the story of our evacuation.

In the 1980's, the American government investigated the treatment of Japanese Americans during this dark episode in the nation's history. Eventually, the U.S. Congress passed a bill that gave some financial compensation to the people who had been in the camps and their descendants. The report that led to this action said:

The evacuees were . . . held in camps behind barbed wire and released only with government approval. For this course of action no military justification was proffered. . . . It follows from the conclusion that there was no justification in military necessity for the exclusion, that there was no basis for the detention.

One group of American immigrants — the Japanese — had suffered a terrible wrong, but now at least the injustice was acknowledged, and an attempt was made to correct it.

*Some Japanese American soldiers were killed in action. This memorial service for some of them was held at the Gila River Relocation Center in Arizona.*

There were cheers in New York City's Times Square on May 7, 1945, as World War II ended in Europe. However, there were millions of displaced persons in Europe by that date, and some of them came to the United States.

# CHAPTER 28: POSTWAR IMMIGRATION AND McCARTHYISM

When World War II ended, marriage was in the news. Thousands of American soldiers had married while overseas, especially in England. The War Brides Act of 1945 provided for the spouses of U.S. soldiers to come to the United States. Between April and July of that year, 44,775 new wives, 61 husbands, and 721 children immigrated to the United States. More wives and children followed before the act expired in 1948.

Refugees—called displaced persons—were also in the news. Some 8 million Europeans awaited repatriation or settlement in countries not their own. The Displaced Persons Act of 1948 helped some of these people come to the United States. By 1961, about 715,000 refugees had entered the United States, mostly under the Displaced Persons Act. These people came as quota immigrants. Countries with small quotas were permitted to mortgage their future allotments—some into the twenty-first century.

War-bride and refugee legislation added to the jumble of immigration laws that Congress had passed since 1924. Over the years, a great number of executive orders issued by the President, laws that covered special cases or problems, and other rules and regulations related to immigration had accumulated. As a result, a special Senate subcommittee was created in 1947 to study the history, legislation, and policies of American immigration and to recommend whatever changes seemed necessary.

The subcommittee took on tasks similar to those the Dillingham Commission had tackled in 1907, with two exceptions. First, the subcommittee investigated all aspects of the displaced persons problem. Second, the subcommittee evaluated the degree to which Communist infiltration and subversion posed a problem for Amer-

The Red Scare of the 1950's. By 1950, the fear of worldwide Communism had reached a point in America that was equal to that of the general fear experienced in 1919 and 1920. In 1945, a clerk in the Soviet Embassy in Ottawa, Canada, sought political asylum in the West. Some documents he brought with him indicated that a few people in the Canadian government had been giving secret information about the atomic bomb to the Soviet Union. President Harry S. Truman established the Loyalty Review Board to make sure that the same situation

> By 1950, the fear of worldwide Communism had reached a point in America that was equal to that of the general fear experienced in 1919 and 1920.

ica. It was the avowed aim of Communists to overthrow the government, and American laws prohibited entry to people with such aims. Therefore, it was surmised that any Communist must have entered the country illegally. So the subcommittee was ordered to investigate:

> the extent, if any, to which aliens have entered the United States in violation or circumvention of [immigration] laws and the extent, if any, to which aliens have been permitted to remain or have remained in the United States in violation or circumvention of such laws.

Deteriorating relations with the Soviet Union, a wartime ally, and the resulting Cold War were the reasons for the study.

did not exist in the United States. From 1947 to 1951, about 3.2 million government employees were investigated. About 200 people whose loyalty appeared questionable were dismissed. Almost 3,000 other people resigned, either because they did not want to be investigated or they felt the investigation violated their constitutional rights.

In 1949, Communist revolutionaries triumphed in China, and the following year, Communist North Korea invaded South Korea. Under the auspices of the United Nations, the United States and many other nations sent troops to repel and drive back the aggressors. In October 1950, China came into the war on North Korea's side. A negotiated peace finally ended the "police action" three years later.

# McCarthyism

cCarthyism. In the meantime, Republican Senator Joseph R. McCarthy of Wisconsin established himself as America's foremost Red-hunter. Actually, his principal interest may have been in gathering headlines for himself.

McCarthy had first been elected to the Senate in 1946. His voting record established him as a friend to segments of the building industry that opposed federal public housing and as a big help to a soft-drink company in need of sugar, which was a scarce commodity for a time. In 1950, McCarthy began to cast about for an issue he could ride to reelection. He found it in what the public perceived as Communism's internal threat to America, and for four years, McCarthy led an investigation whose ruthlessness has seldom been exceeded in the U.S.

However, McCarthy did not invent the Red scare of the 1950's. Fear of Communism had been almost constant in America since the Russian Revolution in 1917. For many, this fear was confirmed in the 1930's and 1940's by the activities of such groups as the House Committee on Un-American Activities. McCarthy capitalized on that fear—to his great political advantage.

In a Lincoln Day speech in West Virginia on Feb. 9, 1950, McCarthy said that he had a list of 205 individuals in the U.S. Department of State who were Communists or Communist sympathizers. The statement was widely reported in newspapers and received a lot of public attention. McCarthy went on to make similar charges in other parts of the country. He kept changing the numbers, though, and did not divulge any names until much later. Even then, he named only individuals whose cases had already been resolved.

However, McCarthy's lack of proof did not diminish his sudden popularity, and he won reelection

*Joe McCarthy was finally brought down, in large part by the televised hearings in 1954 about Communists in the U.S. Army. During the hearings, Army counsel Joseph Welch, left, did much to show the whole nation that McCarthy believed himself to be above the law.*

easily in 1952. He then created his own Senate subcommittee to give himself greater power—and a public forum—to investigate the supposed spread of Communism in America.

The American public seemed more interested in inflammatory accusations than in real proof. The huge public support made McCarthy a powerful political figure as he accused secretaries of state and other government officials of being "soft on Communism." McCarthy even badgered the Republican Administration of President Dwight D. Eisenhower with charges of harboring Communist sympathizers.

At the time, the Communist Party of the U.S.A. had only about 24,000 members, not nearly enough people to be a great political force. However, many people were willing to believe that a large number of Communists operated in secret. Furthermore, because most Communists advocated violent change, many Americans were convinced that any group that promoted any change that might be even remotely called left wing was Communist or at least under Communist influence—and therefore a threat to America.

The McCarthy era contributed a word to the language: *McCarthyism*, the practice of making public and sensational accusations of disloyalty or corruption, usually with little or no proof or with doubtful evidence. McCarthyism affected thousands of people, and ruined many careers in the 1950's. Librarians, college professors, government officials, entertainers, journalists, ministers, and many others came under suspicion. Some industries, such as the movie industry in Hollywood, Calif., *blacklisted* people accused of Communist associations, so that they were boycotted in the industry and unable to get work. To keep their jobs, people in some industries were forced to take loyalty oaths.

One immigrant film star who was greatly affected by the witch hunt for Communists was Charlie Chaplin.

Born into a poor family in London, Chaplin came to the United States in 1910. His stardom began in 1914, when he first appeared in silent movies as "the Tramp," a jaunty, comic character who bounced back from every defeat. In 1919, Chaplin was one

*In 1920, Charlie Chaplin starred with Jackie Coogan in "The Kid." More than fifty years later, the two men were reunited at the ceremony where Chaplin received his honorary Oscar.*

of the four founding partners of United Artists film corporation.

Chaplin lived in the United States for four decades, but he never became an American citizen. In the late 1940's, controversy arose about Chaplin's personal life, and some people also accused him of supporting Communism. In 1952, while he was traveling in Europe, the U.S. government said that he could not reenter the country unless he agreed to participate in hearings about his personal life and political views. Chaplin decided not to return, and he settled in Switzerland. Finally in 1972, Chaplin returned to the United States to accept an honorary Oscar that praised him:

> for the incalculable effect he has had in making motion pictures the art form of this century.

The collapse of Joe McCarthy's power and influence came almost as abruptly as A. Mitchell Palmer's had back in 1920. In 1954, McCarthy accused the U.S. Army of "coddling Communists." The result was a live, nationally televised Senate investigation. About 20 million people watched the 36 days of testimony. McCarthy's performance revealed him to be arrogant, opportunistic, and abusive, and his support evaporated. The Senate condemned him for "contemptuous" conduct toward one subcommittee that had investigated his finances in 1952 and for his abuse of another subcommittee that had recommended he be censured.

The McCarran-Walter Act. In 1952, with McCarthyism at its height, Congress passed an immigration law called the Immigration and Nationality Act, which came to be known as the McCarran-Walter Act. The name referred to Pat McCarran, a senator from Nevada who had chaired the 1947 subcommittee on immigration, and Francis E. Walter, a congressman from Pennsylvania. McCarran was known as an immigration restrictionist, and his anti-Communist credentials were sound. He had also authored the Internal Security Act of 1950, which made it unlawful to plan any action that might lead to the establishment of a totalitarian dictatorship in the United States. President Harry S. Truman had vetoed the measure, saying that people should be punished for the crimes they commit, not their thoughts. However, Congress had overridden the veto.

The McCarran-Walter Act *codified*, or systematized, many of the immigration laws and regulations that had been passed over the years, but

Communist party or other totalitarian party; aliens who advocate the principles of Communism and totalitarianism; and aliens who are members of organizations required to register under the Subversive Activities Control Act [Internal Security Act]. . . .

President Truman vetoed the McCarran-Walter Act. He praised the parts of the act that provided for the general revision of immigration laws and that pertained to immigration from Asia. His objections, however, were more numerous.

Truman objected to the retention of the national origins system, calling it unfair to immigrants from southern

---

# The immediate postwar years also saw the immigration of a large number of people from Puerto Rico . . .

---

the act retained the national origins quota system based on the 1920 census. Protestant and Catholic groups, the Congress of Industrial Organizations, and others had lobbied against the national origins system, but to no avail.

The McCarran-Walter Act also listed 31 categories of people who could be denied entry to the United States. Most of these categories had been established previously, but a few groups were added. The new groups included people who had been convicted of certain crimes twice and people convicted of selling narcotics. Still another group was:

aliens who are anarchists, advocate or teach opposition to organized government, are members or affiliated with the

and eastern Europe. Truman pointed out that the national origins system had made special legislation necessary so that refugees could be admitted after the war. He also objected to parts of the law that forbade entry to people who had been convicted of certain crimes. He pointed out that there were vastly different standards of justice in different countries, among other things. The President also said that the McCarran-Walter Act gave the attorney general too much power in the determination of which immigrants to exclude, the surveillance of immigrants once they were in the country, and the deportation of *aliens*, or people who were not citizens, without appropriate checks. Congress ignored Truman's objections and easily overrode his veto.

However, people opposed to the national origins system did not give up. They continued to lobby Congress on behalf of a change in that aspect of the immigration law. Finally, the Immigration Act of 1965 eliminated national origins and placed all countries on a more equal basis.

# Immigrants from the Caribbean.

The immediate postwar years also saw the immigration of a large number of people from Puerto Rico, an island in the Caribbean Sea. Puerto Rico had become a U.S. possession following the Spanish-American War in 1898, and the United States had granted citizenship status to its people in 1917.

Puerto Rico had been a Spanish colony for hundreds of years, and its economy was anchored in the production of sugar cane, with tobacco as a second major crop. There were jobs available, but most were low-paying farm jobs, and the island's economy did not thrive. By the late 1940's, the average annual income in Puerto Rico was about $300. The generally high birth rate meant that an increasing number of people competed for the few good jobs available.

When World War II ended in 1945, the great demand for consumer goods in the United States stimulated industrial production but also created a shortage of workers. Many Puerto Ricans decided to move to the mainland to take advantage of the job opportunities. The chance to earn $40 a week plus fringe benefits was highly attractive.

In addition, there were relatively low airfares available, and certainly a plane ride of a few hours from San Juan, Puerto Rico, to New York City was an attractive way to make the trip. A person could board an airplane in San Juan at 11 p.m. and arrive in New York City after a 1,600-mile (2,575-kilometer) flight in time for breakfast.

In 1940, about 70,000 Puerto Ricans lived in the United States, nearly all of them in New York City. Fifteen years later, more than 500,000 Puerto Ricans lived in New York City, and another 175,000 had settled in cities such as Chicago and Philadelphia.

The United States fulfilled the Puerto Ricans' desire for jobs, and at expected wages, too. Puerto Ricans found jobs mostly in light manufacturing, as clothes pressers and sewing-machine operators in the garment industry, for example, and worked in service industries as busboys, dishwashers, hospital orderlies, laundry workers, and household servants. However, these jobs rarely led to better ones, and even skilled workers often had to take them.

Most Puerto Ricans did not speak English at first, since people in Puerto Rico speak Spanish. The language barrier prevented many skilled workers from getting good-paying jobs, as had happened to many other non-English speaking immigrants before. In addition, the people already in many trade unions opposed offering membership to the newly arrived Puerto Ricans. The plumbers, carpenters, and electricians did not care for any additional competition. In the face of such opposition, some Puerto Ricans started their own businesses, including repair shops, beauty parlors, and grocery stores.

Wages of $40 per week seemed like a lot when viewed from Puerto Rico, but that income did not go very far in New York City. It wasn't enough to pay for decent housing along with other necessities, so many Puerto Rican immigrants—just like so many other earlier immigrant groups—found themselves living in slums, just as many had lived in back home. They were not financially better off at all.

In New York City, most Puerto Rican immigrants settled on Manhattan's Upper East Side in an area that came to be known as Spanish Harlem. Its broken windows, defective wiring, poor plumbing, little heat, sparse hot water, and rats became a part of the Puerto Rican way of life.

In the cities, Puerto Ricans also had to deal with racial discrimination, which they had not known on their island. About 25 per cent of the Puerto Rican arrivals were African Americans, the descendants of African slaves that the Spaniards had brought to the "New World" centuries before. White Americans tended to treat this group as inferior to themselves and exhibited the same prejudice toward these blacks that they had displayed toward other blacks for so long. Indeed, some whites looked down upon all Puerto Ricans.

Discouraged or homesick, thousands of Puerto Ricans returned to their island home. Still, migration to the mainland continued at a rate of about 40,000 people annually for several years. Despite the obstacles they faced, many Puerto Ricans managed to become a permanent part of the American scene.

The Puerto Rican picture was not completely dark. By the 1960's, about 75 per cent of those working in New York City were semiskilled blue-collar workers, office workers, and

sales clerks. They had managed to move up the economic ladder from the unskilled jobs at the bottom. Also, Puerto Ricans owned more than 6,000 small businesses in the city, including grocery stores, barber shops, and dry-cleaning establishments. In addition, many young Puerto Ricans had begun to find the money needed to attend college, particularly the City University of New York.

Like other immigrant groups before them, the Puerto Ricans left a cultural mark on their new home. Spanish-language newspapers—especially *La Prensa*, the most popular paper published in Puerto Rico—began appearing on New York City news-

*Many Puerto Rican immigrants moved to New York City and started small businesses, such as this family-owned grocery store in a neighborhood called Spanish Harlem. Like many New Yorkers, immigrants from Puerto Rico often live in five- or six-story apartment buildings where there is little surrounding grass and few trees.*

stands. Spanish-speaking radio and television stations started operating in various cities. Restaurants began serving such Puerto Rican specialties as *asopao*, a chicken or seafood stew with rice and vegetables. People celebrated the feast days of San Juan and other saints.

Thus ended another era of American immigration. The close of World War II led to immigrant brides and immigrant refugees. However, the era also saw the rise—and fall—of a self-serving politician whose witch hunt for Communists hurt both immigrants and native-born alike. At the same time, the era saw the large-scale immigration of new and special groups such as the Puerto Ricans, who were already American citizens.

# PART 10: RECENT YEARS

In the late 1800's, a change in the places of
origin of most immigrants had led to the term *new
immigrants*. After World War II, another shift
prompted the term *new, new immigrants*. Many of
America's new, new immigrants came from Asia,
Latin America, and other areas that had been relatively
underrepresented in the past. Above all, the question
"What is an American?" now had more answers than
ever before.

*Today, America's
naturalized citizens
come from countries
all around the globe.
At this 1988 Citizen-
ship Day ceremony
on Ellis Island, one
person from each of
50 countries became
an American.*

*In the early 1900's, some Asian immigrants, such as these Filipinos in California in 1936, could find work only as farm laborers. Later, after World War II, other Asian Americans, such as Senator Daniel Inouye, right, became national leaders.*

# CHAPTER 29: NEW IMMIGRANTS FROM ASIA AND LATIN AMERICA

A large community of Japanese Americans had developed in Hawaii before World War II, and immigration from Japan to Hawaii resumed after the war. When Hawaii became a state in 1959, Japanese Americans became an important political force in all levels of government. This was especially true after the Immigration and Nationality Act of 1952, also known as the McCar-

ran-Walter Act, allowed the *Issei*, or first-generation Japanese immigrants, to become citizens. Before long, half the members of Hawaii's legislature were Japanese Americans. Hawaiians also sent Spark Matsunaga, Patsy Takemoto Mink, and Daniel Inouye to Congress in Washington, D.C.

Both Matsunaga and Inouye had won Purple Hearts in World War II as members of the famous 442nd Army Battalion made up of Japanese Americans, and both men later served as commanders of the Disabled American Veterans in Hawaii. Daniel Inouye was first elected to the U.S. Senate in 1962. Spark Matsunaga served several terms in the House of Representatives before being elected to the Senate in 1976.

After 1945, many American soldiers stationed in occupied Japan

*Like other immigrants, Asian Americans have integrated parts of their cultural heritage into American life. The Chinese gate marks one entrance to San Francisco's Chinatown, and a woman, above, in Hawaii practices the Japanese tea ceremony.*

married Japanese women. After the occupation ended in 1952, about 25,000 Japanese war brides came to the United States. In the 1960's and 1970's, about 70,000 more Japanese immigrants came to America. Like many of their predecessors, those who were unskilled often became gardeners. However, many of the recent arrivals were white-collar workers and skilled professionals. The Japanese-American population became large enough to support television programs in Japanese in Honolulu, Hawaii; San Francisco; Los Angeles; and New York City.

Another readily apparent Japanese influence in the United States can be seen in the restaurant industry. New York City, Chicago, San Francisco, and other large American cities have hundreds of restaurants that serve Japanese specialties such as *sashimi*, or raw fish; *sukiyaki*, which consists of beef strips, vegetables, and noodles cooked rapidly in a soybean and sugar sauce; and *tempura*, which consists of vegetables, seafood, or meat dipped in batter and fried in deep fat. During much of the 1980's, Japanese food was very popular and Japanese restaurants were considered to be quite chic by many people.

Chinese. Once the quota system was abolished in the 1960's, Taiwan, Hong Kong, and China itself also contributed to American immigration. Many of the new Chinese arrivals were educated urban people who tended to settle in the Chinatown areas of New York City, San Francisco, Los Angeles, and Chicago. By 1980, about 500,000 Chinese Americans lived in the United States, with more than 50,000 of those living in Hawaii alone. Both San Francisco and New York City had more than 100,000 Chinese-American residents each.

*Like many other immigrants, Chinese Americans enjoy celebrating their cultural heritage.*

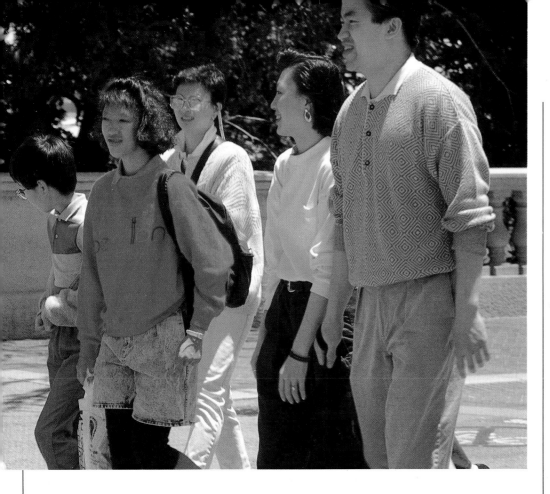

*Many Korean American children take their classes seriously because their families place a high priority on education.*

**K**oreans. The end of the Korean War in 1953 led to the first great wave of Korean immigration to the United States. Like the immigrants who arrived after World War II, most of these arrivals were war brides. By the 1960's, many Korean immigrants to the United States were university professors, scientists, doctors, and other white-collar workers. Most of them settled in cities such as Los Angeles, where the Korean population jumped from about 5,000 in 1970 to about 150,000 in 1980.

Once in the United States, though, Korean immigrants did not always do the same type of work as they had done in Korea. In many cases, both husbands and wives took whatever jobs they could find and saved their money until they had enough capital to open a restaurant or grocery store. By 1980, Korean Americans ran about 6,000 small businesses of various kinds in Los Angeles. In El Paso, Tex., the number of Korean retail stores grew from just 1 in 1982 to 30 in 1985. By the late 1980's in New York City, Korean Americans owned and operated about 80 per cent of all the fruit and vegetable businesses in town.

Many Korean Americans have started small retail businesses in areas with large black populations, and in some areas, violent clashes erupted between the two groups. In New York City in early 1990, for example, a black woman accused a Korean grocer of pushing her to the ground and accusing her of shoplifting. Other African Americans picketed the store, and the dispute eventually brought the mayor to the scene in an attempt to defuse the controversy.

Many of the difficulties have arisen because of cultural differences between the two groups. As the head of the Korean American Small Business Service Center of New York Inc. pointed out, "In Confucian culture we don't smile very much and women are taught not to touch men so they put the change on the counter." In other words, Korean shopkeepers were not being rude; they were simply

*In December 1983, Indian-born Subrahmanyan Chandrasekhar received the Nobel Prize for physics from Sweden's King Carl Gustaf at a ceremony in Stockholm. Chandrasekhar and fellow American William A. Fowler shared the award for their work done on the evolution and death of stars.*

behaving the way they had been taught to behave. In addition, what African Americans perceived as hostility was often really just a poor command of the English language or fatigue at working up to 16 hours a day. In their own defense, Korean Americans also pointed out that 60 per cent of the food they carried in their grocery stores—such as crabs, mangoes, and yams—came from black suppliers in Haiti, Jamaica, and Trinidad.

In the summer of 1990, tensions rose in Chicago's Roseland neighborhood when African Americans accused some Korean merchants of treating them all as potential shoplifters and seeming to display indifference when serving them. In addition, there were complaints that Korean retailers took money out of the community and gave nothing back. As in New York City, some African Americans picketed various Korean-owned stores. The Korean merchants responded by citing high crime rates in the neighborhood and pointing out that they needed to provide jobs for members of their own families before they could hire people from the neighborhood. The dispute was settled when the Korean merchants agreed to deposit some of their money in neighborhood banks, to institute more liberal refund policies in their stores, and to participate in neighborhood improvement projects.

**Asian Indians.** In 1980, the U.S. Bureau of the Census counted almost 390,000 immigrants from India in the United States. Five years later, estimates placed the number at more than 500,000, and since then, more than 25,000 Indian immigrants have come to America in most years. In general, the Indian immigrants are middle-class professionals, including many doctors, business people, and university professors.

One famous, and relatively early, immigrant from India is Subrahmanyan Chandrasekhar, co-winner of the 1983 Nobel Prize for physics. Early in his career, Chandrasekhar wrote a paper that predicted the existence of *black holes* in the universe. A black hole is an area so dense that not even light can escape the pull of its powerful gravitation. Chandrasekhar came to the United States in 1937, when he joined the faculty of the University of Chicago, and he became an American citizen in 1953.

# Filipinos.

The United States acquired the Philippine Islands as a consequence of the Spanish-American War of 1898. The islands then received colonial status, and their residents were free to move to the United States. In the early 1900's, many Filipinos found work as unskilled laborers in the United States or in Hawaii.

In 1935, the United States granted commonwealth status to the Philippines. In part, this action was taken to satisfy Filipino demands for independence, but it also satisfied the demands of America's agricultural industry and labor unions. Agricultural interests wanted to keep Filipino exports of hemp, sugar, and copra from coming into the country. Labor unions wanted to keep out foreign workers during the Great Depression of the 1930's. As a result, the Philippines were assigned a quota of only 50 immigrants per year.

World War II interrupted the Philippines' transition to independence, which finally arrived on July 4, 1946. Then, the Philippine quota was raised to 100 immigrants per year. Af-

*Many Filipino American doctors and nurses now work in hospitals across the United States.*

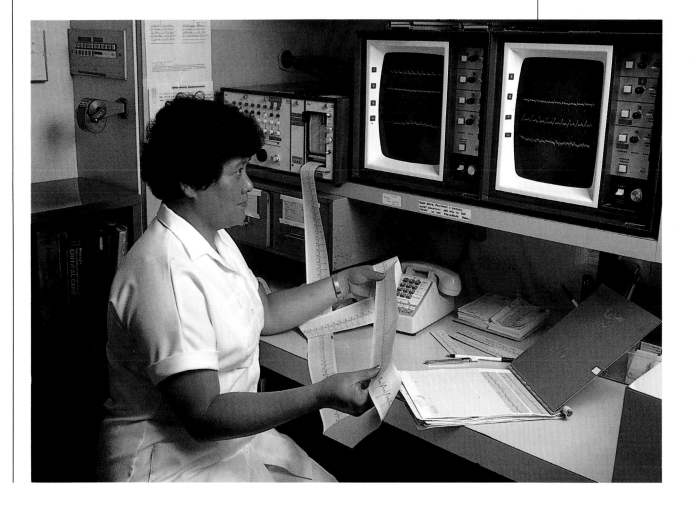

ter the lifting of the quota system in 1965, however, thousands of Filipinos came to the United States. A total of 355,000 Filipino immigrants arrived between 1971 and 1980. In the 1980's, 50,000 to 60,000 Filipinos came to America each year.

Filipino immigrants settled mainly in Hawaii and on the U.S. west coast. Although many Filipino immigrants could only find low-paying jobs, other Filipinos were technical workers or highly trained professionals. By 1980, more than 9,000 Filipino doctors lived in the United States—compared with 13,000 in the Philippines itself—and thousands of Filipino nurses worked in hospitals in Chicago, San Francisco, and Los Angeles. Filipino nurses were welcomed in American hospitals because they received al-

most the same training as U.S. nurses, and America has a serious shortage of trained nurses.

**Dominicans.** The Dominican Republic covers the eastern two-thirds of the Caribbean island that Christopher Columbus named Hispaniola. During the 30-year dictatorship of Rafael Leonidas Trujillo Molina, emigration from the Dominican Republic was severely curtailed. Following Trujillo's assassination in 1961, however, restrictions were loosened, and thousands of Dominicans came to the United States seeking a better life. By 1980, at least 300,000 Dominicans resided in the United States, and about 60 per cent of them were recent immigrants. During the last half of

*Celebrated fashion designer Oscar de la Renta was born in the Dominican Republic, learned his craft in Europe, and came to the United States in the 1960's.*

the 1980's, about 25,000 immigrants from the Dominican Republic arrived in America each year.

The Dominican immigrants, who settled mainly in urban areas of Florida and the Northeastern United States, came from nearly all economic levels and worked in a wide variety of occupations. The game of baseball is very popular in the Dominican Republic, and several baseball players such as George Bell and Pedro Guerrero were recruited by American teams, often at salaries of hundreds of thousands of dollars per year.

most South American immigrants to the United States. At the beginning of World War II, less than 2,000 Colombians lived in the United States. Many of them were professionals, and in New York City, they had established their own community in the Jackson Heights neighborhood. This neighborhood continued to be a center for middle-class Colombian immigrants as their numbers gradually increased after the war.

Between 1945 and 1955, some 8,000 Colombian immigrants came to the United States. In 1960 alone,

> Over the years, the number of immigrants from the nations of South America has been steady but not large in comparison with the great waves of newcomers from other nations.

**P**eoples of South America. Over the years, the number of immigrants from the nations of South America has been steady but not large in comparison with the great waves of newcomers from other nations. Between 1910 and 1930, immigrants from South America averaged about 4,000 a year. During the 1970's, first- and second-generation South American immigrants totaled about 350,000 people, with most living in cities of the Northeast and in Chicago, Los Angeles, and San Francisco. Immigration from each country has varied considerably, but Ecuador, Argentina, and Colombia have supplied the most people.

The experience of Colombian immigrants is probably much like that of

another 3,000 Colombians arrived. These newcomers included many farmers, artisans, and other workers who had few job prospects and also suffered from the effects of political turmoil in Colombia. By 1970, New York City had about 27,000 first- and second-generation Colombian immigrants. Most came from the urban areas of the Colombian highlands. In New York City, they established their own churches, professional and social clubs, and other institutions. About 3,500 other Colombians settled in metropolitan Chicago. These people were mainly from the area of Colombia along the Caribbean. Many were white-collar professionals such as medical doctors, engineers, and accountants. Like other middle-class, educated professionals, they soon prospered.

The largest in area of all the 50 states, Alaska is the only one with borders that touch two other nations—Canada and the Soviet Union—but none of the other 49 American states.

# ALASKA

Its huge area and relatively isolated geographic position have caused it to have a somewhat different history than most of the rest of the United States.

### Early Years.
Alaska's first people were part of the great migration across the Bering Land Bridge about 20,000 years ago. Among those who settled on the mainland and some coastal islands were the groups that became known as the Tlingit, Tsimshian, and Haida. Probably arriving later, the Aleuts occupied the harsh, windswept string of islands known as the Aleutians. People that came to be known as Eskimos settled along the northern edge of Alaska and in some areas of the interior.

Many centuries passed before other people came to this land. Then in 1728, Vitus Bering, a Danish explorer working for Russia's Czar Peter the Great, reached Saint Lawrence Island, which is now part of Alaska. Bering and his party sailed through the Bering Strait, which now bears his name, between Asia and North America. However, they did not see the North American mainland because of severe fog. In 1741, Bering and Russian explorer Aleksei Chirikov led a second expedition that landed on what is now Kayak Island.

### Life in the 1800's.
One result of these early explorations was the founding in 1799 of the Russian-American Company, which traded mostly in sea otter furs. Alexander Baranof was the company's first manager, and he treated the Indians quite harshly. In 1799, the Tlingit Indians rose up in revolt and killed or captured most of the Russians living at the company's settlement near what is now Sitka. In 1802, Baranof in turn attacked and defeated the Tlingit. He then founded the settlement of New Archangel (now Sitka), and it soon became the largest town in Russian America.

Until 1817, the Russian-American Company prospered. However, it declined after that for two reasons. First, Baranof, the harsh but successful manager, was replaced by Russian naval officers who had little interest in commercial affairs. Second, the Russian fur business now had

This sketch of an Alaskan native was done by a Russian in the 1800's.

Life was harsh for people of the Russian-American Company, including Alexander Baranof, left. At least for a while, however, the sacrifice seemed to be worthwhile because the seal hunting, shown above in an 1828 Russian sketch, was quite successful.

some competitors—the Americans, the Canadians, and the British.

By the 1850's, the Russian government had taken over most of the Russian-American Company, but the government had bigger problems to attend to. The major problem was the Crimean War from 1853 to 1856. As a result of this war, Russia needed money, and Czar Alexander II found a way to get it. In 1867, Russia sold Alaska to the United States of America for $7.2 million, or about 2 cents per acre (5 cents per hectare). On March 30, 1867, U.S. Secretary of State William H. Seward signed the Treaty of Cession of Russian America to the United States.

At home, some U.S. newspapers derided the purchase and said that it was worthless. They called it *Seward's Folly* and *Seward's Icebox*. However, other Americans thought the purchase was a good one, and they favored the acquisition. Near the turn of the century, they were proved right when gold was discovered, first near Nome in 1899, and

One of the first gold strikes in Alaska was made by Felix Pedro, left, and led to the founding of Fairbanks. Like other towns, such as Dawson City, above, Fairbanks was a bustling, expensive, and sometimes muddy place to live in the 1800's.

Alaska is the largest state in the union in area, but one of the smallest in population.

Arctic Ocean

Barrow

Nome

Fairbanks

CANADA

Anchorage

Juneau

Bering Sea

Pacific Ocean

Missionary John Chapman was also a photographer who documented much of the Indian way of life in the late 1800's and early 1900's.

World War II brought big changes to Alaska, though. Because Alaska is so close to Asia, it was important militarily in the war with Japan, and at one time 152,000 U.S. troops were stationed in Alaska. In 1942, Japanese troops captured some of the Aleutian Islands, making them the only part of North America to be invaded during the whole war.

In 1958, Congress voted to admit Alaska, and President Dwight D. Eisenhower issued a proclamation on Jan. 3, 1959, declaring it to be the 49th state in the union. In some ways, this made for tougher economic times in Alaska, but the 1968 discoveries of major oil deposits helped to change that.

However, Alaska's population continued to be small, especially considering the state's huge land area. By 1980, the state's population was less than 402,000 people. Of these, 50,000 were Eskimos and 24,000 were Indians. Many of the rest of the people were born in states other than Alaska. Today, Alaskans celebrate their ethnic diversity and far-flung origins with a variety of unique holidays such as Russian Christmas, the Little Norway Festival, and the World Eskimo-Indian Olympics.

Today, Alaska's economy depends heavily on petroleum production, as shown below. The development of this industry has caused people from many other states to migrate to Alaska. Fishing, especially along the southern coasts, is also an important industry.

then near Fairbanks in 1903. These discoveries attracted more people to the area and aroused more interest in Alaska in the "lower 48."

**Life in the 1900's.** Finally in 1912, the U.S. Congress passed a law that made Alaska a U.S. territory and provided for a territorial legislature. However, Alaska's population remained relatively small and even declined somewhat between 1910 and 1920.

Hawaii is the only state in the union that does not lie on the mainland of North America, and it is also the southernmost state. It is made up of 132 separate islands, but almost all the peo-

from Tahiti arrived in Hawaii and took control from the earlier settlers.

On Jan. 18, 1778, James Cook, a British sea captain, and his crew landed in Hawaii. Cook named the islands the Sand-

Soon, though, Hawaii became a stopping point for many European ships. The ships brought livestock, manufactured goods, and plants from other countries. However, the ships also brought diseases that the Hawaiians had not known before. As with the Indians in the Americas, many Hawaiians died from smallpox, measles, diphtheria, and other diseases.

**James Cook sailed along the coast of Alaska and also visited Hawaii.**

# HAWAII

ple live on seven of the eight main islands at the southeastern end of the chain.

### Early Years.
Hawaii became a land of immigrants about 2,000 years ago when the Polynesians sailed there in gigantic canoes. About A.D. 1200, another Polynesian group

wich Islands in honor of the Earl of Sandwich, the first lord of the British admiralty. Cook traded with the Hawaiians, who treated him well. However, in February 1779 during a second visit, Cook was stabbed to death in a fight between his crew and some of the island's people.

### Life in the 1800's.
In the late 1700's, Hawaii had a bloody 10-year civil war that ended when Kamehameha, the chief of one of the islands, got control of most of the other islands and proclaimed the Kingdom of Hawaii.

King Kamehameha I greatly increased foreign trade. He also kept alive the old customs and religion of his people. However, shortly after he died, Protestant missionaries from the United States

**After he unified the islands, King Kamehameha I kept alive the old ways of his people by encouraging the continued use of traditional double-hulled canoes, such as this one from the era.**

A Belgian priest, Damien Joseph De Veuster, shown in this statue, improved conditions for people in the leper colony on Molokai.

arrived, and they soon converted most of the Hawaiians to Christianity.

During the middle of the 1800's, Hawaii became a melting pot of people from vari-ous countries. There were not enough Hawaiian workers for the plantations, so the owners of the great sugar cane fields brought in workers from other countries. In the 1850's, many Chinese workers arrived. In 1859, the first Polynesians from the South Pacific came, and in 1868, the first Japanese workers came, as did Portuguese workers in the 1870's.

During the late 1800's, sugar cane planting and pineapple growing became big businesses on the islands. About the same time, Hawaii got a new ruler, Queen Liliuokalani I, who tried to restore some of the power of the monarchy. Liliuokalani also was less sympathetic to business interests than her predecessors had been.

In 1893, Liliuokalani was overthrown in a bloodless revolution led by nine Americans, two Britons, and two Germans. The group also had the help of some American sailors and marines who landed to keep the peace.

One of the revolt's leaders, Sanford Dole, became president of the Republic of Hawaii and asked the United States to annex the islands. U.S. President Grover Cleveland felt that the Americans in Hawaii had involved the United States in a dishonorable action, and he tried to prevent the annexation. However, the United States annexed the islands in 1898 anyway, after

Also a songwriter, Queen Liliuokalani wrote the well-known *Aloha Oe.*

Grover Cleveland was out of office. Sanford Dole served as Hawaii's first territorial governor, from 1900 to 1903.

By the 1900's, Hawaii's population included a broad mix of immigrants, including Portuguese farm workers and these newspaper boys from a variety of ethnic backgrounds.

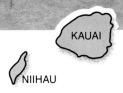

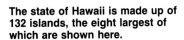

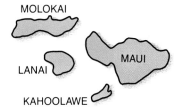

**The state of Hawaii is made up of 132 islands, the eight largest of which are shown here.**

### Life in the 1900's.

American business and military interests controlled events in the islands in the early decades of this century. At the same time, several bills calling for Hawaiian statehood were introduced into the U.S. Congress. Most of these bills were not even voted on because many members of Congress feared that the thousands of Asian Americans in Hawaii might not support the United States in a war. However, this fear proved to be without foundation, as shown by events of World War II.

On Dec. 7, 1941, Japan attacked the U.S. naval base at Pearl Harbor and the U.S. airfields at Oahu. The United States suffered heavy losses in lives, ships, and aircraft, but the restored bases later played a key role in the U.S. campaign against the Japanese. In 1949, the National Memorial Cemetery of the Pacific was dedicated. Thousands of American military personnel are buried there and at the U.S.S. *Arizona* Memorial nearby.

On Aug. 21, 1959, Hawaii became the 50th state. During the next decade, its population grew more than 20 per cent, and its economy boomed, especially in the area of tourism.

Hawaii now has a population of about 1 million people, of which only about 15 per cent are of chiefly Hawaiian ancestry. The rest of the population comes from a rich diversity of ethnic backgrounds. In fact, many Hawaiians take pride that everyone is part of a minority. Said one ethnic Hawaiian, "People get along here because everyone celebrates everyone else's holidays."

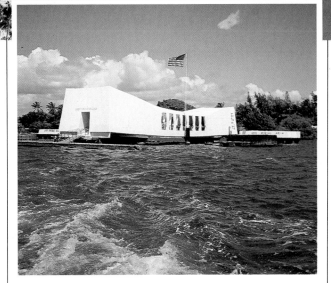

**Today, tourism is Hawaii's main industry. Waikiki Beach in Honolulu is a major tourist haunt. Many tourists also visit the memorial to the U.S.S. *Arizona*, which was sunk on Dec. 7, 1941, at the start of World War II.**

Soviet immigrant Walter Polovchak, above, and his family came to the United States in search of freedom from oppression. When his parents decided to return to the U.S.S.R., Polovchak, then a teenager, went to court to gain the right to remain behind.

# CHAPTER 30: FLEEING POLITICAL OPPRESSION

For centuries, immigrants have come to America to escape oppression. During colonial times, religious minorities such as the Puritans, Quakers, Mennonites, Amish, and Huguenots fled Europe for a land in which they could more freely worship in the way that they chose. Political change, such as the French Revolution, also stimulated immigration to the "New World," and

Many Nicaraguan immigrants are children, left, some of whose parents were killed in their war-torn homeland. The poverty of postwar Vietnam brought the U.S. other refugees, who left their country in small boats, risking drowning.

failed revolutions such as those in Germany and Austria-Hungary in the 1840's drove many former rebels to leave those regions.

Late in the 1800's, *pogroms* (massacres) in Russia and in Russian-held territories drove 2 million Jews from their homelands. Many came to the United States. These Jews still faced some prejudice, but they were allowed to enter the country. However, the United States government did not establish an enviable record of aid to Jews in the 1930's when anti-Semitism spread through Nazi Germany and the countries that Germany took over. After the war, though, America accepted hundreds of thousands of Jews and other refugees.

# Hungarians, Czechs, and Poles.

After World War II, Communist believers, with the backing of the Soviet Union, took control of the governments in many Eastern European countries. Hungary was among the nations that suffered this fate.

In October 1956, street fighting broke out in the capital city of Budapest as the Hungarian people rose up in revolt against their Communist government and the economic and political oppression it had caused.

tural and industrial production had dropped, and there were general shortages of food and other goods. Communist Party leaders criticized the government for failure to reverse the nation's economic decline, and Czechoslovak intellectuals called for more freedom of expression. At the same time, ethnic Slovaks renewed their efforts to gain rights as a minority group in the nation. The party removed Antonín Novotný as party secretary in 1968 and replaced him with Alexander Dubček, a Slovak.

Dubček liberalized the government and allowed greater freedom of the press and more contacts with non-Communist nations in what came to be called the Prague Spring. Dubček's

## In 1956, more than 30,000 Hungarian refugees emigrated to the United States.

Within days, Soviet troops and tanks poured across the Hungarian border and put down the rebellion. At the time, American immigration laws permitted only 5,000 Hungarian immigrants per year, but President Dwight D. Eisenhower issued an executive order and changed that ruling. In 1956, more than 30,000 Hungarian refugees emigrated to the United States. Eventually, about 200,000 Hungarians left their homeland as refugees. Like their predecessors in 1848, many of these people immigrated to the United States and joined the hundreds of thousands of people of Hungarian descent already living in America.

In 1968, similar events occurred in Czechoslovakia. Communists had taken over the government there in 1948, and by the early 1960's, agricul-

government proved highly popular with the people, but it also turned out to be short-lived.

In August 1968, fearing a weakening of Communist control in Czechoslovakia and apprehensive that people in other Eastern Bloc countries might demand similar reforms, the Soviet Union invaded Czechoslovakia. Dubček was replaced, and tight government controls were reinstated. Just as in Hungary, the failed effort created large numbers of political refugees. A lot of them eventually settled in the United States. Other Czechs also wanted to leave the country, and many who could, did.

Martina Navratilova, who was born in Prague in 1956, was one who decided to leave. In 1975, she defected to the United States during a tennis tour. She became an American citizen six years later. Navratilova won many tennis championships, including a record of nine All-England (Wimbledon) Championships as well as the French Open, the Australian Open, and the United States Open. For several years, she was ranked as the number one woman tennis player in the world.

In the early 1980's, a wave of liberalization, encouraged by the popular Solidarity movement, swept the nation of Poland. Decades of economic mismanagement and decline finally brought the workers at Lenin Shipyards in Gdańsk to rise up in protest, led by an electrician named Lech Walesa. The popular revolt failed at that time, and several thousand Poles managed to leave the country, including many who came to the United States. The story of Poland has a happier ending, however. In 1989, the Communist government of Poland fell, and the new government embarked on a stringent program of economic reforms.

One emigrant from Poland to America has had a distinguished career in political science. Zbigniew Brzezinski came to the United States in 1953 and was naturalized in 1958. He served as assistant to President Jimmy Carter on national security affairs from 1977 to 1981. He acted as Carter's chief adviser on defense and as head of the National Security Council. In 1987, he became a member of the President's Foreign Intelligence Advisory Board, and in 1989, he became a professor of International Studies at Johns Hopkins.

Like the government of Poland, other Communist governments fell in Eastern Europe in 1989. These independence movements, along with the reunification of Germany in 1990, seemed to eliminate those nations as

*Czechoslovakian-born Martina Navratilova, who defected to the United States in 1975, is one of the world's top women tennis players.*

*In 1985, Mikhail Baryshnikov, center, starred in the movie* White Nights *with fellow dancer Gregory Hines. The plot concerns a Russian defector, played by Baryshnikov, who accidentally returns to the U.S.S.R. after a forced airplane landing.*

future sources of political refugees. Still, the poor economic conditions of these countries meant that other reasons for wanting to emigrate remained.

**S**oviet Jews. Throughout history, the Jews in Russia, and later the Soviet Union, have faced persecution. After World War II, thousands of Jews wished to emigrate, but the government threw up numerous barriers. For a time, Jews could leave only after paying an "educational tax," which was figured as the cost to the state of that person's education. In some cases, the tax amounted to thousands of dollars. In addition, even an

expressed desire to emigrate was enough to cast suspicion on an individual's loyalty. It could even be a black mark against that person's boss at work.

The number of Jews permitted to leave the Soviet Union varied from year to year and seemed to depend on the mood that happened to prevail among Soviet leaders at the time. Between 1966 and 1977, about 130,000 Soviet Jews were allowed to emigrate. About 15,000 of these people came to the United States. Most of the other Jewish emigrants went to Israel. Then in 1990, as if to underscore the unpredictability of Soviet policy, the Soviet government allowed 200,000 Jews to emigrate to Israel alone. This was nearly as many as had been allowed to emigrate during the previous 42 years since Israel was established.

Most Jews left the Soviet Union in family groups, generally headed by well-educated professionals. In the United States, they settled in Baltimore, Boston, Chicago, Philadelphia, and Los Angeles. Many also settled in Brighton Beach, a section of New York City.

# Soviet Defectors.

Soviet dancers, musicians, and athletes found that getting permission for a tour abroad or to participate in an international competition was almost as difficult as emigrating. When traveling in Western countries, such groups were closely watched to prevent any individual from defecting. Despite the precautions, though, some did defect. Three such defectors were Rudolf Nureyev, Natalia Makarova, and Mikhail Baryshnikov, all of whom were ballet stars at the height of their careers.

Baryshnikov, the last of the three defectors, was born in the Soviet city of Riga, Latvia, in 1948. He started his training in ballet at age 12, and within 7 years, he had become a soloist with the famous Kirov Ballet of Leningrad. While on tour in the United States in 1974, Baryshnikov defected and soon joined the American Ballet Theatre (ABT) in New York City. In 1980, he became the artistic director of the ABT, a position he held for most of the decade.

Natalia Makarova defected to the West in 1970 and lived in the United States for many years. She danced with the American Ballet Theatre from 1970 to 1972, and later, she appeared as a guest star with other ballet companies around the world. After she retired from the ballet stage, she wrote her autobiography, founded her own ballet company, and starred on Broadway in a musical comedy called *On Your Toes*, which had first been produced on Broadway in 1936. The play concerns the life and times of a Russian ballet star who has fled to America. For her performance, Makarova won the 1983 Tony award for best actress in a musical.

# Soviet Exiles.

In some instances, the Soviet Union forced artists into exile. The best-known such artist is Soviet novelist Alexander Solzhenitsyn.

Solzhenitsyn first got into trouble in 1945 as an officer in the Soviet army, when he made an adverse comment about Stalin, the Soviet leader, in a letter to a friend. He was arrested and spent eight years in a prison labor camp and three years in internal exile. Solzhenitsyn's book *One Day in the Life of Ivan Deniso-*

*Novelist Alexander Solzhenitsyn, shown here with his wife, settled in the United States in 1976.*

354

*When tensions somewhat eased between the U.S.S.R. and the United States, Mstislav Rostropovich and the National Symphony Orchestra briefly toured the Soviet Union and played concerts in Leningrad and Moscow in the late 1980's.*

*vich* deals with life in a Soviet prison camp. In 1962, the Soviet government published the book without censoring it, a most unusual event, and it received good reviews.

Following that success, Solzhenitsyn wrote *Cancer Ward* and other works. All these works won wide critical acclaim, and in 1970 Solzhenitsyn won the Nobel Prize for literature for his work. At the same time, though, Solzhenitsyn often spoke out against various Soviet policies, particularly censorship. In 1973, he published the first volume of *The Gulag Archipelago*, a title that referred to the system of prison camps spread across the Soviet Union. Solzhenitsyn had

written the book some years before, but he decided to publish it in the West after a copy fell into the hands of the Soviet police.

In *Gulag*, Solzhenitsyn recounted horrible experiences in camp prisons in rich detail—naming names and specifying places. He also brought down a fire storm of official Soviet criticism on himself, not only for *Gulag*, but for all his works.

In the spring of 1974, shortly after the first volume of *The Gulag Archipelago* had been published in Paris, the Soviet government stripped Solzhenitsyn of his citizenship and exiled him from his homeland. Later, his family was allowed to join him in

Switzerland, where they lived for about two years. In 1976, the family settled in the United States. In 1990, the Soviet Union offered to restore Solzhenitsyn's Soviet citizenship, but he refused it.

The Soviet Union accorded much the same treatment to the well-known conductor and cellist, Mstislav Rostropovich, and his wife, opera diva Galina Vishnevskaya, who had defended Solzhenitsyn publicly. The two were dismissed from their positions in the Soviet musical world, relieved of their citizenship, and exiled. In 1977, they settled in the United States, where Rostropovich became conductor of the National Symphony Orchestra in Washington, D.C.

During a turnabout under the regime of Mikhail Gorbachev in the late 1980's, the Soviet Union welcomed the Rostropovichs back, restored their citizenship, and invited them to contribute to Soviet music once again. The two musicians visited their old home, but they returned to the United States.

Immigrants from Southeast Asia. In 1957, a revolt began against the South Vietnamese government. Soon, the rebels were aided by the Communist regime in North Vietnam. In an attempt to prevent the spread of Communism, the United States aided South Vietnam and finally sent hundreds of thousands of troops. Despite U.S. efforts, though, North Vietnam emerged victorious in 1975.

Fearful of their future under a Communist regime, thousands of South Vietnamese sought to leave the country. Before the fall of Saigon, South Vietnam's capital city, 65,000 South Vietnamese were airlifted out of the country by the departing Americans. An equal number also found their own ways to escape, many of them to neighboring Thailand. Thousands of others left over the next three years. By 1978, about 170,000 Vietnamese refugees had settled in the United States.

*During the Vietnam War, there were many babies born to Vietnamese mothers and American fathers. Le Thi Lien, shown here, is one. Her mother died when she was 3 months old. She and her adopted family would like to come to the United States.*

One famous Vietnamese immigrant is Nguyen Cao Ky, the flamboyant former South Vietnamese air force general and, later, prime minister. After he arrived in the United States, Ky settled in southern California and started a small business.

The end of the Vietnam War was not the end of the upheavals in Southeast Asia, though. In 1975, a brutal Communist group called the Khmer Rouge took over Cambodia. The Khmer Rouge forced most Cambodian people out of their city homes and into the countryside to work as farmers, eventually killing hundreds of thousands. The killing stopped only after Vietnam invaded Cambodia and drove out the Khmer Rouge in

that they were unable to care for the refugee boat people and tried to send them back. Other countries turned them away when they tried to land.

By 1985, about 700,000 people from Vietnam, Cambodia, and Laos had been admitted to the United States. After that, about 40,000 more immigrants arrived each year. Many came from Vietnam under an arrangement that had been worked out between the government there and the United States.

The first such immigrants arrived in America in 1975, and they were often well-educated people who spoke English and had many associations with Americans in their homeland. Among them were former govern-

> ## The Khmer Rouge forced most Cambodian people out of their city homes and into the countryside to work as farmers, eventually killing hundreds of thousands.

1979. A Communist government also took over in Laos.

Hundreds of thousands of Cambodians and Laotians joined the Vietnamese and thousands of ethnic Chinese in fleeing the Southeast Asian nations. Some made their way to refugee camps in Thailand. Others became so-called boat people who were so desperate to leave that they set out in small, overcrowded boats on dangerous sea voyages, seeking refuge in Thailand, Hong Kong, the Philippines, or Malaysia. Many boat people fell victim to pirates or storms, and often, those who arrived safely were not welcomed. Some countries insisted

ment officials, civil servants, and professional people. Many of these immigrants had an easier time adjusting to a new land than did the boat people who followed. Many boat people had made their living by farming or fishing, and they were not well educated and knew little or no English. Like countless immigrants before them, they not only had to learn a new language but also had to become familiar with the many other aspects of a new culture. Most of the first arrivals eventually settled in the states of California and Texas.

Some Vietnamese in Texas worked in the fishing industry, as they had in Vietnam. Prices for crab and shrimp were low at the time, and fuel costs were high. The Vietnamese immigrants caused further cuts in the incomes of the established fishers, and arguments eventually escalated into violence. In 1979, one person was killed during a fight between the two groups. Vietnamese immigrants to California seemed to have a somewhat easier time during their first few years in America.

Another ethnic group of refugees that came to the United States from Southeast Asia are the Hmong. In their own language, their name means *free people*, and they are believed to be descended from the soldiers of Genghis Khan, a Mongolian leader whose armies established the world's largest empire during the 1200's. About 200 years ago, the Hmong were forced out of China into northern Laos, where they became

farmers. They were hard-working but had no written language. In fact, they did not even use the wheel until World War II. During the Vietnam War, they helped the Americans and resisted the Communists. As a result, when North Vietnam won the war, the Hmong fled through the jungles to Thailand. From there, about 100,000 came to the United States.

Life in America has been difficult for the Hmong. There is not only the language barrier. There are cultural differences, too, such as the fact that Hmong men usually have several wives. The Hmong have benefited from their tradition of close family and clan ties, though. Members of the same clan live near each other and help each other to adjust to a new way of life. One result is that Hmong youngsters do very well in school, because doing poorly means they would bring shame to their families.

*Many Hmong immigrants have worked very hard to learn English and other aspects of American life.*

*Numerous Cuban immigrants have settled in Miami, Fla., where there are many signs of the Cubans' cultural and linguistic heritage.*

# Cubans.

In 1959, rebels led by the fiery revolutionary Fidel Castro overthrew the long-time dictatorship of Fulgencio Batista in Cuba. At first, the United States recognized the new Cuban government, but trouble soon arose when Castro proceeded to establish a Communist government. In 1961, the United States formally severed diplomatic relations with the tiny island nation.

Direct airplane flights between Cuba and the United States continued to operate until 1962, however, and the Castro government did little to stop people who wanted to leave. As a result, about 155,000 Cubans left their island home. The majority of these emigrants were middle-class professionals, such as doctors, lawyers, engineers, and business people who had a great deal to lose under a Communist regime. Many skilled and white-collar workers also left Cuba for the United States. Direct flights resumed in late 1965. Until they ended once again in 1973, about 257,000 Cubans immigrated to the United States.

In 1980, with Castro's permission, about 125,000 more immigrants, mostly young men, left Cuba for the United States. Most of the refugees traveled on a vast flotilla of ships and boats provided by friends and relatives in the United States. Because they left Cuba from the port of Mariel, these immigrants became known as marielitos.

Mixed in among the 125,000 marielitos were nearly 3,000 criminals and people with severe mental illnesses. After prolonged negotiations, Castro in 1984 agreed to take many of this group back and soon accepted about 400. However, about 2,500 people remained in American prisons or other institutions, and about 100 were still in American mental institutions. Dealing with the marielitos, the Cuban boat people, cost the United States about $2 billion. The marielitos had arrived suddenly, mostly in south Florida. Such a large number of immigrants all at one time severely taxed the U.S. immigration system.

When the marielitos first arrived, they were sent to temporary refugee camps located at military bases in Arkansas, Florida, Pennsylvania, and Wisconsin. Cubans with relatives in the United States were able to leave the camps fairly soon. Those without relatives, however, sometimes remained in the camps for up to a year. There was no privacy and nothing to do in the camps, and people in nearby communities were extremely hostile. One result was the outbreak of riots in which hundreds of refugees set fires and threw stones at military guards as a protest against the crowded conditions and the slow rate at which they were being processed.

The majority of the 700,000 or so Cubans in the United States reside in Florida, mainly in Miami, where they transformed the city's social, economic, and political climate in one generation. The Cuban immigrants were not all members of the middle class, nor did they all achieve that status in America. Many Cubans settled into low-paying, unskilled jobs. Still, the numerous individual success stories of Cuban immigrants added to the general population's perception of them as resourceful, aggressive, and energetic people.

In 1985, the people of Miami elected Xavier Suarez, a Cuban immigrant, as their mayor. In the race, Suarez defeated another Cuban, Raul Masvidal. In 1981, Cuban refugee Raul Martinez had been elected mayor of the nearby city of Hialeah. In 1986, immigrant Bob Martinez was elected governor of Florida.

# Haitians.

Haiti, on the western third of the island of Hispaniola not occupied by the Dominican Republic, was a poor country almost from its inception as a nation in the early 1800's. The country endured continual political turmoil as coup followed coup and dictators came and went.

As a result, many more Haitians wanted to come to the United States than could legally do so under the

*The 1980's saw the election of hundreds of Hispanic Americans as state officials, among them Miami mayor Xavier Suarez, shown here with reporters after his victorious 1988 mayoral election.*

*After making a long and dangerous sea voyage in open boats, these Haitian immigrants rejoiced at reaching the United States safely.*

U.S. Immigration Act of 1965. In the 1970's, several thousand Haitians tried to flee their island home for the United States, hoping to be accepted as political refugees. Many Haitians drowned when their ramshackle, leaky boats sank, and others died of exposure on the way.

The United States government refused to allow the Haitian boat people to enter the country as political refugees, insisting that they had come for economic reasons. Would-be Haitian immigrants were detained pending deportation proceedings. Many were poor, it was true, but many also fled Haiti's dictator, known as Baby Doc, and his dreaded secret police—the *Tontons Macoutes* (bogeymen). The reason for the U.S. refusal of these

boat people might have been that the United States valued the Haitian government's anti-Communist attitude and did not wish to acknowledge officially that a friendly government persecuted its citizens. In any case, the number of Haitians trying to enter the United States gradually dropped off. However, by 1980 about 300,000 Haitian immigrants lived in the United States, mainly in Boston, New York City, Chicago, Miami, and Washington, D.C.

**Nicaraguans and Guatemalans.** In 1979, rebels in Nicaragua overthrew the 42-year dictatorship of the Somoza family. A Marxist guerrilla group known as the *Sandinistas* headed the new government, but soon it too faced a rebellion. This time the rebels were mostly former Somoza supporters and others who eventually became known as the *contras*, meaning *those against*.

Declaring that the Sandinistas planned to establish a Communist regime in Nicaragua, the United States supported the contras with weapons and financial aid—a move that aroused much controversy in the United States. In the meantime, rebel guerrilla warfare began against right wing governments in neighboring Guatemala and El Salvador.

The United States supported the governments of both Guatemala and El Salvador and refused to accept people fleeing those countries as political refugees. At the same time, the U.S. government opposed the Nicaraguan government, but it would not allow most Nicaraguans to enter America as political refugees either. In 1984, for example, only 305 Nicaraguans, 105 Salvadorans, and 17 Guatemalans were granted political asylum in the United States.

However, many refugees from Nicaragua, Guatemala, and El Salvador entered the United States illegally. In many cases, these people received aid from religious groups in the United States and others who were opposed to the American government's policies. It was estimated that by the late 1980's, nearly half of the Central Americans in the United States had entered the country illegally. Many had traveled first to Mexico and then headed north across the Rio Grande into the United States. In 1986, the U.S. Immigration and Naturalization Service (INS) changed its policy, at least with respect to immigrants from Nicaragua, and decided to grant asylum to some people based on specific rules and regulations. The INS granted asylum to about half of the Nicaraguans who requested it.

*Not all people who make it to the United States are allowed to stay, as is the case with these Guatemalan refugees who were photographed outside an INS detention center near Bayview, Tex.*

*Like many immigrant groups, Mexican Americans enjoy celebrations of their ethnic heritage. This mariachi band concert in San Francisco commemorated a Hispanic holiday called Cinco de Mayo.*

*Mexican Americans, both famous and little-known, now play major roles in American life.*

# CHAPTER 31: LATIN AMERICAN IMMIGRANTS AND UNDOCUMENTED WORKERS

Victory in the Mexican-American War in 1848 gave the United States a Spanish-speaking population. Mexico ceded California and other parts of the West and Southwest to the United States as part of the Treaty of Guadalupe Hidalgo. At that time, there were about 80,000 Mexicans in the area, mainly in California and New Mexico. Today, there are more than 12 million people of Mexican ancestry in the United States. Most of them live in urban areas in California and the Southwest, but cities in the Middle West and the East have large populations with Mexican ancestry.

# Mexican Immigrants.

Mexicans—both residents of the United States and those who came from Mexico to take temporary jobs in the 1800's—were instrumental in building southwestern railroads, such as the Santa Fe and the Southern Pacific, for which they usually earned $1 to $1.25 per day. Many were employed as miners and as cowboys and shepherds on cattle and sheep ranches. These workers were extremely valuable during the labor shortage of World War I, bringing in the harvests as migrant workers.

The restrictive immigration laws of the 1920's did not apply quotas to Mexican immigrants, and the demand for Mexican labor continued strong. This freedom of entry was requested by agricultural interests that wanted to employ migrant laborers. Things changed during the Great Depression of the 1930's when millions of Americans were unemployed and willing to do agricultural work even for low wages. About 500,000 Mexicans, half of them United States citizens, were returned to Mexico, not unlike the earlier situation where American citizens were deported during the Red Scare.

People of Mexican ancestry endured much prejudice and discrimination in the Western United States, and they were not encouraged to assimilate into mainstream America. Prejudice was especially strong in California and Texas, where segregated housing led to segregated, poorly funded schools for their children. In Texas, food shops sometimes refused to serve Mexican Americans, and churches held separate services "For Colored and Mexicans." In Arizona, schools and movie theaters were segregated so that Mexican Americans would not be seated with Anglos.

Some Mexican immigrants used art and theater both to express their resentment over the prejudice they encountered and to help develop pride in their background. For example, in

Santa Fe, N. Mex., a group of folk artists—Los Artos Guadalupanos de Aztlan—began covering the walls of the city's buildings with murals that portrayed Aztec gods and such Mexican independence fighters and reformers as Father Miguel Hidalgo.

Poet Luis Valdez created El Teatro Campesino among the migrant farm workers of the San Joaquin Valley in California. The actors—all of them farm workers—wore masks and signs explaining their characters—such as *ROTTEN GRAPE* or *ESQUIREL*, meaning strikebreaker.

World War II again brought a labor shortage, and once more Mexicans were called on for help. The United States and Mexico worked out a plan that allowed Mexican workers to enter the United States on a temporary basis. Mostly, they harvested crops and returned to Mexico when the harvest was over.

Altogether, about 5 million Mexican workers participated in the plan.

*This mural in East Los Angeles, Calif., honors the heritage of Mexican Americans. Called* Ghosts of the Barrio, *it blends historical figures, such as a Spanish* conquistador *and a Mexican revolutionary, with ordinary people of today.*

Wages and annual incomes were low—30 cents per hour and about $500 per year—but there was no shortage of applicants.

The original program that allowed Mexican laborers into the United States ended in 1947. It had been especially beneficial to the owners of large farms who pointed out that the Mexican workers helped keep grocery prices low. The farm owners' lobbying kept the program alive until 1964, when it was finally closed out due to increased mechanization of the harvest, a mandated $1-per-hour wage, and publicity about the wretched working and living conditions. Owners of large farms and the American public had not been the only beneficiaries. The money that the Mexican workers took back to Mexico added some $200 million to that nation's economy.

In 1965, immigration laws placed a 20,000 ceiling on the number of visas that could be issued to immigrants from any one country in a year. In some countries, including Mexico, this resulted in a long waiting list for visas.

By the 1950's in California, Mexican Americans made up 20 per cent of the auto workers, about 50 per cent of

building trades union members, and a large number of garment-industry workers. The number of Mexican Americans in professional and technical occupations increased steadily, too. However, percentages in those fields varied widely from state to state. By 1970 in New Mexico, for example, 9.7 per cent of all Mexican-American men and 10 per cent of all Mexican-American women were employed in technical and professional jobs, compared with 5.4 per cent of Mexican-American men and 7.4 per cent of Mexican-American women in Texas.

Since the mid-1980's, there has been a shift in immigration from Mexico. Nowadays, most immigrants come intending to stay in America rather than to work for just a few months and then return to Mexico. Also, today's immigrants are often families with children instead of single men. In addition, more and more immigrants come from Mexico's cities as opposed to its rural areas, and once in the United States, they look for work in a city rather than on a farm. As a result, certain urban businesses in the United States—car washes, hospitals, hotels, laundries, and restaurants—have come to de-

*Today, Mexican Americans are found in a wide variety of leadership roles. In Chicago, Mario Aranda was first a university professor. Later, he became executive director of the city's Latino Institute. Lena Guerrero formerly served as a Texas state representative and is now the state railroad commissioner.*

*The shallow Rio Grande, which forms most of the U.S.-Mexican border, is no obstacle to many of the unknown thousands of Mexicans who enter the United States illegally every year.*

pend on Mexican immigrants to fill their low-paying jobs.

Mexican-American representation in political office has not been widespread, though there have been some successes in recent years. In 1985, Richard Alatorre became the first Mexican American elected to the Los Angeles City Council. Also in the 1980's, Henry Cisneros became the first Mexican-American mayor of San Antonio, Tex.

**Undocumented Workers.** Increasingly difficult economic times in Mexico drove many potential immigrants to take desperate steps. Sometimes they entered the United States illegally. These people came to be called *undocumented workers*, meaning that they did not have the legal documents to prove they had entered America by legal means. Undocumented workers from many Central American countries journeyed through Mexico and crossed the border into the United States. However, the majority of the undocumented workers were Mexicans.

The Mexican-U.S. border is a long one and impossible to secure without an army of law enforcement officials. As a result, many people tried to cross into the United States at that point. Some unscrupulous individuals offered—for a fee—to guide the undocumented workers across the border and to their destinations along the safest routes. However, these guides often exploited the undocu-

to lose but a labor force that could be replaced easily. In the meantime, an employer could take advantage of workers who feared discovery of their illegal status and therefore did not object to long hours, low wages, and poor conditions.

Attention began to focus on undocumented workers in the 1970's. In 1978, Congress created the Select Commission on Immigration and Refugee Policy to study the issue. The Commission held hearings throughout the nation, consulted experts, conducted research projects, and analyzed the results. In 1981, it filed a 13-volume report.

---

# Increasingly difficult economic times in Mexico drove many potential immigrants to take desperate steps.

---

mented workers. Many travelers died in highway accidents or perished of thirst after being abandoned in the desert.

Once in the United States, most undocumented workers ended up in low-paying service jobs, such as busboys, dishwashers, hotel maids, and janitors. Some undocumented workers found jobs as unskilled laborers on construction projects and in small factory operations.

Many undocumented workers "documented" themselves by buying counterfeit papers that indicated they had entered the United States legally. With or without such "proof," though, these workers were easy prey for exploitative employers. The U.S. government did not require employers to check that their employees were legal residents, so an employer with illegal aliens on the payroll had nothing

Deciding how many undocumented workers were in the United States was a large task in itself, and estimates ranged from a low of 2 million to a high of 12 million. The commission finally estimated the number of undocumented workers at between 2 million and 4 million.

Many immigration experts contended that the undocumented workers took jobs that citizens and legal residents did not want, and therefore the undocumented workers were important to the U.S. economy. However, the commission decided otherwise. It concluded that undocumented workers replaced American workers in some service industry jobs and manufacturing enterprises. Furthermore, the commission said that the undocumented workers drove down wages and working standards in some regions.

*Many undocumented workers came from Mexico to find seasonal employment in California's huge agricultural industry.*

versy. It recommended that penalties be imposed on employers who hired undocumented workers. Congress had never seriously considered this before, and opposition to the idea now arose from several sources.

Many Mexican-American leaders opposed the idea because they believed that employers would discriminate against people who looked or sounded foreign, rather than risk being penalized. Both the Chamber of Commerce of the United States and some agricultural organizations also opposed the idea because they felt it might drive many companies who hired foreign workers out of business.

Finally, the commission recommended that once sanctions were in place, all undocumented workers who had entered the United States before a certain date should be granted *amnesty*, or pardon, and be given the right to apply for legal status. This idea was also controversial because it seemed to reward people who had broken the law. Amnesty also seemed unfair to the many people who had waited years for their legal entry visas.

Some people concluded that no laws granting amnesty or measures to strengthen the border guard would solve the problem. They believed that undocumented workers would continue to cross the border until the economies of Mexico and many Central American nations improved and jobs were available in their homelands for all workers who wanted them. However, considering the high birth rates, depressed economies, and difficult political situations in many such nations, that day might be a long time in coming.

The commission also decided that the constant fear of discovery caused many problems for undocumented workers. In order to avoid official detection, these workers did not report crimes, avoided seeking health care, and did not send their children to school. Nor did they try to learn English or attempt to upgrade their skills by registering for night classes or other educational programs.

One commission recommendation stirred up considerable contro-

A bill that included many of the commission's recommendations was introduced into Congress in 1983. It was sponsored by Republican Senator Alan K. Simpson of Wyoming and Democratic Representative Romano L. Mazzoli of Kentucky. In late 1986, Congress finally passed the Immigration Reform and Control Act. The law set penalties for employers who hired undocumented workers and offered amnesty to many undocumented workers. The bill also provided for the seasonal importation of 350,000 foreign workers per year to harvest perishable fruits and vegetables if not enough American workers were available.

Under the amnesty provision, undocumented workers who could prove they were in the United States before Jan. 1, 1982, would be granted resident alien status. Undocumented workers seeking amnesty were given until May 4, 1988, to apply. About 3.1 million people did.

Unfortunately, it soon became clear that the problem had not been solved entirely. Counterfeiters continued to do a brisk business in fake social security cards, immigration papers, passports, and driver's licenses — documents usually accepted as proof of a person's right to work in the United States. Fake social security cards were sometimes sold for as little as $20, while a document showing that a person had completed the first

step toward citizenship might cost as much as $500. Employers were required to demand documentation of a worker's legal status, but they did not have to authenticate the papers that workers presented. In some instances, employers actually referred prospective employees to places where they could buy such falsified documents. Immigration officers might locate, arrest, and convict the people who sold the phony documents, but tracking down the actual counterfeiters who made them frequently proved to be a difficult task. So the problem of undocumented workers continued to be a vexing one for all those involved. In 1991, a U.S. Supreme Court decision meant that as many as 100,000 additional undocumented workers may be granted legal status. Ira Kurzban, a lawyer who represented several thousand of these workers said, "It's probably the most significant immigration case in the last quarter-century." Surely, decisions about immigration will continue to be an American issue for many years to come.

*Some undocumented workers, such as this couple in Austin, Tex., were pleased to apply for the U.S. amnesty program. Others, however, were reluctant because they feared they would be denied amnesty and deported.*

*Children dressed to represent America's multiethnic population often march in parades that celebrate the nation's freedom. This freedom is also symbolized by the Statue of Liberty.*

# CHAPTER 32: AMERICAN MELTING POT, AMERICAN PLURALISM

In 1751, Benjamin Franklin deplored the ways of German immigrants to establish separate communities and keep intact language, customs, and traditions of their homeland. Pennsylvania was, after all, an English colony, noted Franklin, but the German communities were becoming so numerous that they threatened "to Germanize us, instead of our Anglicizing them."

*Pride in individual heritage and participation in baseball— the national pastime—are two ways that Americans celebrate who they are.*

Franklin believed that all immigrants should assimilate into the predominantly English culture.

Thirty years later, essayist Michel-Guillaume Jean de Crèvecoeur expressed a different point of view in his famous *Letters from an American Farmer:*

[An American] is either a European or the descendant of a European, hence that strange mixture of blood, which you will find in no other country. I could point out to you a family whose grandfather was an Englishman, whose wife was Dutch, whose son married a French woman, and whose present four sons have four wives of different nations.

Crèvecoeur spoke of individuals as being "melted into a new race of men," thus suggesting the "melting pot" theory of immigration.

The Bubbling Cauldron. During most of the 1800's, western and northern Europeans continued to dominate American immigration. The melting pot idea seemed to prevail, although no one then used that expression. The term was popularized in 1909 by a stage play entitled *The Melting Pot* and written by Israel Zangwill, a British playwright.

David, the play's hero, is an idealistic young Jew who wants to eliminate "Old World" nationalities in the United States and favors the creation of an American nationality that would be new and superior to the others, where "all races and nations come to labor and look forward." The play was

grants shed every trace of their previous life in the process of becoming Americans. Having thus taken on a repressive, nativistic tone, the idea of a melting pot fell into disrepute.

Greektowns, Little Italies, Chinatowns, Spanish Harlem, and other ethnic communities remained. While retaining many of their cultural characteristics, though, new immigrants became Americans in much the same way immigrants had in the past. As comedian Harpo Marx noted, the relationships immigrant kids had with other immigrant groups were:

all part of the endless fight for recognition of foreigners in the process of becoming Americans. Every Irish kid

> While retaining many of their cultural characteristics . . . new immigrants became Americans in much the same way immigrants had in the past.

not a critical success. However, its ideas struck a popular chord, and the play enjoyed a long run.

*The Melting Pot* appeared on the stage just as concern was growing over the huge numbers of immigrants from southern, eastern, and central Europe that were arriving in America. Many people considered these new immigrants to be "unmeltable," or unable to assimilate into American culture. At the same time, an increasing number of programs were offered at such institutions as settlement houses and the Young Men's Christian Association (YMCA) to help newcomers. During World War I, these programs and many others tried to eliminate ethnic differences in an effort to promote national unity. The melting pot idea seemed to demand that immi-

who made a Jewish kid knuckle under was made to say "Uncle" by an Italian, who got his lumps from a German kid, who got his insides kicked out by his old man for street fighting and then went out and beat up an Irish kid to heal his wounds. "I'll teach *you!*" was the threat they passed along, Irisher to Jew to Italian to German. Everybody was trying to teach everybody else, all down the line. . . .

Young immigrants learned to be Americans in schools where they read U.S. history and pledged allegiance to the flag and took part in games and athletics. They learned to be Americans through participation in community activities and on the job. They

learned from radio and the movies, from the music, the slang, and the ways of life favored by young people. Later, they learned from television, music videos, shopping malls, and fast-food outlets.

Many of the first generation of any immigrant group were unskilled and poor, but the second generation acquired skills and gained entry to professions that enabled them to move out of slums. A few of the second generation—but many of the third generation—moved to the suburbs.

In the late 1930's, an emphasis on *cultural pluralism* allowed ethnic groups to keep some of their "Old World" identity. The contributions of various ethnic groups became important as a means of improving intergroup relations and lessening prejudice. During World War II, the government stressed ethnic diversity as a way of reinforcing national unity and emphasizing the idea that people all over the globe were involved in a struggle against tyranny. Many institutions took up this theme, particularly the movie industry. In war movies, a small group of soldiers, a rifle squad, for example, was usually an ethnic mix of soldiers who were Jewish, Irish, Polish, Italian, Chinese, and occasionally Scandinavian along with "old American" types representing the English settlers. However, blacks were conspicuously absent. African Americans who fought in World War II did so in segregated units, just as their fathers and grandfathers had in earlier wars. The melting pot idea had not yet been applied to America's black citizens.

African Americans gained some measure of equality as a result of the civil rights movement that began in the 1950's. African Americans identified themselves as an ethnic group and sought to build self-esteem and pride in their own culture. One way was to urge the inclusion of black history and black studies as well as an

*New York City's Little Italy, above, is the scene for the annual festival of San Gennaro. Summertime always brings numerous ethnic celebrations throughout the country.*

*On Jan. 13, 1990, Douglas Wilder took the oath of office as Virginia's governor.*

emphasis on black accomplishments in the national educational curriculum from elementary school through college. Another way was for blacks to assert themselves politically.

Thousands of black candidates were elected to public office on all governmental levels. African Americans were elected mayor in Detroit, Atlanta, New York City, Chicago, Los Angeles, and many smaller cities. In 1989, Douglas Wilder became the first black governor of Virginia, where blacks make up about 20 per cent of the total population. In 1990, Sharon Pratt Dixon became the first black woman mayor of a large U.S. city and the first woman mayor—black or white—of Washington, D.C.

The **Salad Bowl.** Another term used to describe the intermingling of America's ethnic groups is a *salad bowl.* The melting pot analogy seemed to require people to lose some of their distinctiveness, and take on some of the characteristics of others. In the salad bowl analogy, however, the parts are all mixed together with none giving up any of their distinctive qualities. Instead, they all coexist and enhance one another.

Ethnic pluralism became a valued part of the American scene, and ethnic celebrations took on deeper meanings as members of various ethnic groups—and all Americans—came to relish the celebrations of their ethnic diversity. Irish immigrants and their descendants continued to celebrate St. Patrick's Day with as much zest as ever, and Columbus Day remained as much an Italian holiday as a national one. Firecrackers explode and dragons breathe smoke as Chinatown residents all over the country celebrate the Chinese New Year. African Americans and many others revere Martin Luther King Day.

The residents of Chicago honor Casimir Pulaski, the Revolutionary War hero from Poland, each year on a special day. Mexican Americans annually mark El Cinco de Mayo, while German Americans celebrate Oktoberfest. Everyone celebrates the Fourth of July.

The **Language Controversy.** Today, public signs in many cities are often printed in two languages—Spanish and English. Official documents in some states are also printed in both languages, and in San Francisco, voting instructions appear in Chinese as well. The Los Angeles County courts have skilled interpreters available for 80 different languages. Many stores around the nation post signs reading: "Se Habla Español." Some merchants in neighborhoods with large Hispanic populations display signs saying: "We Speak English." As a nation of immigrants, the United States has always been a place where many different languages could be heard. At least to some extent, an official stamp of approval has been placed on that multilingual heritage.

Some American businesses require their employees to use only English, even in situations that do not involve English-speaking customers. Such rules create controversy and have led to a number of court cases involving the rights of employees.

People who favored language restrictions formed two groups to further their goals—English First and U.S. English. Both organizations favor a constitutional amendment or federal legislation declaring English to be the nation's official language. Some states passed English-only legislation, but most such laws are largely symbolic in nature, or are practically unenforceable.

Official or not, English is the language of most of America. In the past, first-generation immigrants had trouble learning it, but members of the second generation mastered it. Most observers agree that recent immigrants will follow suit.

After World War II, the influx of immigrants from Asia and Latin America left the United States with a greater ethnic diversity than it had ever known before. Some people feared that this diversity would inevitably lead to divisiveness. However, as Lawrence H. Fuchs of Brandeis University pointed out:

What binds Americans to one another, regardless of ethnicity or religion, is an American civic culture. . . . It is a complex of ideals, behaviors, institutions, symbols and heroes connected by American history and its great documents, the Declaration of Independence, the Bill of Rights, the Gettysburg Address. It is backed by a civil religion giving transcendent significance to those ideals. And it is the basis for accepting ethnic diversity while protecting individual rights. An American can be as ethnic as he or she wishes in private actions, but in public actions, the rules of the civic culture are binding.

Becoming a Citizen. Each year, about 125,000 immigrants to the United States go through a process called *naturalization*, in which they become citizens of the United States. The naturalization process involves

St. Patrick's Day in the United States is primarily a nonreligious holiday on which many people—regardless of their heritage—wear green and attend parades.

three steps and is administered by an agency of the Department of Justice called the Immigration and Naturalization Service, or INS.

In the first step, a potential citizen submits an application to the INS, including a fingerprint card, photographs, and a biographical information form. The fee for filing the application is $50.

After the application has been processed, the potential citizen meets with an INS officer for an examination, and two U.S. citizens serve as witnesses. At this point, the potential citizen submits a petition for naturalization. As part of the examination, the applicant must prove he or she meets certain qualifications with respect to age, place of residence, character, loyalty, and education. An applicant must be 18 years old, have lived as a permanent resident in the United States for the previous five years, and have resided in the state where citizenship is being sought for at least six months. Brief departures from the country during the past five years are permissible, and spouses of U.S. citizens may qualify after just a three-year residency.

In addition, an applicant must prove he or she has lived by generally accepted moral standards throughout the last five years. Those considered to be not of good moral character include habitual drunkards, gamblers, adulterers, polygamists, criminals, prostitutes, or drug dealers. A convicted murderer is automatically disqualified.

As to loyalty, a person who had been a member or a willing supporter of the Communist Party during the past 10 years would be disqualified. So would a person who in any way was connected with the Nazi Party between 1933 and 1945.

Finally, as part of the examination a person must demonstrate ability to speak, write, and read ordinary English words and phrases, along with basic knowledge of American history, the Constitution, and the U.S. form of government. The English literacy requirement does not apply to applicants over 50 years old who have been permanent residents for at least 20 years before filing the petition for naturalization.

After the face-to-face examination, INS officers might request additional evidence of an applicant's qualifications. When the investigation is completed, officers prepare a report for the judge who will conduct the final hearing.

For those whose petitions have been accepted, the final hearing is a formality. However, for a person about to become a citizen, the formality is an important one. After citizenship has been granted, the new citizen swears the following:

> I hereby declare, on oath, that I absolutely and entirely renounce and abjure all allegiance and fidelity to any foreign prince, potentate, state, or sovereignty, of whom or which I have heretofore been

a subject or citizen; that I will support and defend the Constitution and the laws of the United States of America against all enemies, foreign and domestic; that I will bear true faith and allegiance to the same; that I will bear arms on behalf of the United States when required by the law; or that I will perform noncombatant service in the armed forces of the United States when required by the law; or that I will perform work of national importance under civilian direction when required by the law; and that I take this obligation freely without any mental reservation or purpose of evasion; so help me God.
If a citizen cannot bear arms or perform noncombatant service because of religious beliefs, he or she may omit those statements from the oath.

A naturalized citizen enjoys all the rights and privileges of natural-born citizens, with one exception. Only natural-born citizens are permitted to be elected President of the United States.

New immigrant citizens cannot make it to the White House, but their descendants can—and have. Tens of millions of people from around the globe have come to America in search of "Life, Liberty, and the pursuit of Happiness." Once here, they have sometimes faced poverty and even prejudice, but they have persevered. The United States of America offered them the opportunity to succeed. Countless millions have taken that opportunity and succeeded—brilliantly.

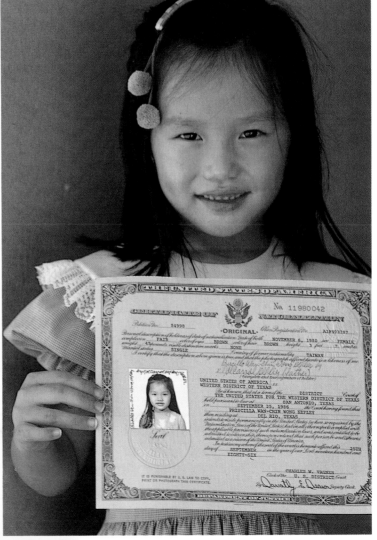

*Citizenship ceremonies, such as this one in San Antonio, Tex., often involve many people taking the oath of citizenship at one time. Children, such as this girl, as well as adults, can become naturalized citizens.*

Four women and four men could be called "immigrants" to a new land without ever leaving America. For two years, they will be sealed inside Biosphere II, a glass-enclosed, self-

## BIOSPHERE II

contained environment covering several acres (hectares) in the desert near Tucson, Ariz.

During their stay, the eight volunteers will carry out various scientific experiments that could have far-reaching applications. The volunteers range in age from 26 to 66 and were chosen from among many applicants. One of the group, Roy Walford, is a medical doctor assigned the task of overseeing the volunteers' diet and health. The other volunteers are scientists, engineers, and computer specialists.

During their 24 months in Biosphere II, the volunteers plan to gather data that will be useful to the construction of earthlike environments on the moon, Mars, or other planets. At the same time, the Biosphere II experiments and observations will address problems of life on earth today, including acid rain, ozone depletion, and global warming.

Earth itself is Biosphere I. Biosphere II is built like a gigantic terrarium and contains seven *biomes*, or major ecosystems, in miniature. One biome is agricultural. It is where the volunteers can grow their own food and raise livestock, including pigs, chickens, and goats. The agricultural biome also has large water

The desert biome, left, of Biosphere II includes a wide array of plants from the cactus family. At night, the illuminated Biosphere II dome, below, can be seen for miles (kilometers) across the Arizona desert.

tanks for fish that the volunteers will eat.

Another biome is desert, patterned after the humid, or "fog," deserts of Baja California. A third biome is swampland, with both salt water and fresh water. A fourth biome is tropical savanna, or grassland. The fifth biome is an "ocean," complete with a lagoon and a coral reef, as well as about 1,000 species of marine life. A mechanism using compressed air and a fan produces waves on the ocean while another creates tides.

The sixth biome is a rain forest with a stream that flows down a mountain. The stream goes through the savanna, the saltwater swamp, the freshwater swamp, and into the ocean.

The seventh biome of Biosphere II consists of living quarters where each of the eight volunteers has an apartment. Offices, a library, laboratories, and a recreational area are also there.

The biomes hold hundreds of animals, including frogs, bats, lemurs, termites, and songbirds. There are in fact about 4,000 animal and plant species in Biosphere II. The animals will supply carbon dioxide needed for photosynthesis, and the plants will furnish the oxygen that animals and humans need to breathe. Energy for photosynthesis and to heat the air of Biosphere II will come from the sun.

Heat from the sun also contributes to a hydrologic cycle. The sun's rays warm the desert air, which collects moisture when it drifts over the Biosphere II ocean. Once above the rain forest, the moisture-laden air cools and falls as rain or dew. The moisture eventually feeds into the stream which carries it back to the ocean to begin the cycle once again.

Many things, including the water of Biosphere II, can be recycled. Waste water, for example, can go through a waste recycling system so that the liquid can be used again for irrigation.

Biosphere II can be observed by tourists. Many of the biomes' walls are glass, and ocean life can be viewed at various depths through underwater windows.

In May 1990, technicians, such as the one above, transferred the reef collections to the ocean biome. The floor plan for Biosphere II shows how the living quarters for the eight volunteers are near the farm they must tend for their food.

Ocean

Saltwater marsh    Freshwater marsh

Rain forest

Savanna

Desert

Living quarters

Farm

# ACKNOWLEDGMENTS

272-74: Excerpt from *Harpo Speaks!* by Harpo Marx, © 1961. Used by permission of Limelight Editions, New York, N.Y.

372: Excerpt from *Harpo Speaks!* by Harpo Marx, © 1961. Used by permission of Limelight Editions, New York, N.Y.

All World Book maps were created especially for this volume by John M. Isard and Roberta Polfus.

177 National Park Service, Gift of Yolanda Talbot (Karen Yamauchi, Meta Form, Inc.)
180 © Owen Franken, Stock, Boston
182 Chicago Historical Society, #1932.18
184 Wadsworth Atheneum, Hartford; National Anthropological Archives, Smithsonian Institution; Washington University Gallery of Art, St. Louis
185 Chicago Historical Society
186 Collection of Mrs. Edmundo Lassalle, New York; New York Historical Society
188 American Antiquarian Society; Marietta College Library
190 Burton Historical Collection, Detroit Public Library
191 Chicago Historical Society; Independence National Historical Park Collection
192 Beineke Rare Book and Manuscript Collection, Yale University
193 Indiana Historical Society
195 Thomas Gilcrease Institute of American History and Art
196 Bettmann
197 Woolaroc Museum, Bartlesville, Oklahoma
200 From *The Bay and Harbor of New York* by Samuel Waugh. Museum of the City of New York; Jimoxi Ostrowski Collection (Steven Mays for Time-Life, Inc.); Minnesota Historical Society
202 Bettmann; Smithsonian Institution, #P-64260-A
204 From *Setting Traps for Beaver* by Alfred Jacob Miller. Joslyn Art Museum, Omaha
205 Frick Art Reference Library
206 Culver
207 Granger Collection; Bettmann
208 © Fred J. Maroon; Bettmann, Bettmann
210 Culver
211 Bettmann
213 New York Public Library; Culver
214 From *The Verdict of the People* by George Caleb Bingham. Art Collection of The Boatmen's National Bank of St. Louis
215 Culver; New York Public Library
217 Bettmann
218 Culver
219 Huntington Library, San Marino, California
220 New York Public Library
221 Museum of American Political Life, University of Hartford; Smithsonian Institution, #60114-B
222 Culver
224 From *Emigrant Train Fording Medicine Bow Creek, Rocky Mountains* by Samuel Colman. Bennington Museum; Homer Garrison Memorial Texas Ranger Museum; South Dakota State Historical Society
225 Denver Public Library
226 From *Stephen F. Austin* by William Howare. Archives Division, Texas State Library
227 Thomas Gilcrease Institute of American History and Art
229 Utah State Historical Society; Edward E. Ayer Collection, Newberry Library
230 © Texas Memorial Museum
231 Archives Division, Texas State Library
232 Granger Collection
233 Anschutz Collection
234 Utah State Historical Society
236 Statens Museum for Kunst, Copenhagen; Utah State Historical Society
238 Levi Strauss & Co.; California State Library
239 California State Library; Bettmann
242 National Park Service. From *Bull Run Battlefield* by James Hope. In THE CIVIL WAR: *First Blood* © 1983 Time-Life Books Inc. (Lon Mattoon); Society of California Pioneers; Southern Historical Collection
243 Historical Pictures Service
244 Granger Collection

245 Historical Pictures Service
246 New York Historical Society; Western Reserve Historical Society
247 Scotts Bluff National Monument, National Park Service; Union Pacific Railroad
248 Massachusetts Commandery Military Order of the Loyal Legion and the U.S. Army Military History Institute; Library of Congress
249 Kansas State Historical Society
251 Granger Collection; Historical Pictures Service; Western History Department, Denver Public Library
252 Culver
254 Alfred Stieglitz Collection, National Gallery of Art; New York Historical Society
255 Culver
257 Brown Bros.
258 Minnesota Historical Society
259 Library of Congress
260 Brown Bros.; Culver
261 Brown Bros.
262 Culver; American Museum of Immigration, Statue of Liberty National Monument; National Park Service, Gift of Yolanda Talbot (Karen Yamauchi, Meta Form Inc.)
263 Comstock
264 Culver
265 Brown Bros.; E. L. Wilson and W. I. Adams, 1876, Bibliothèque du Conservatoire National des Arts et Métiers, Paris
266 Library of Congress
267 Brown Bros.
268 American Museum of Immigration, Statue of Liberty National Monument
269 California Department of Parks and Recreation
270-271 © Andrew Popper, Picture Group
272 Brown Bros.; Alice Austen; International Museum of Photography at George Eastman House
273-274 Brown Bros.
275 Culver
276-277 Brown Bros.
278 New York University; Culver
279 Culver; Brown Bros.
280 Culver; Jacob A. Riis Collection, Museum of the City of New York; Amalgamated Lithographers of America, New York
281 Jane Addams Memorial Collection, University Library, University of Illinois at Chicago
282 Smithsonian Institution
283 Culver
284 Brown Bros.
285 Jacob A. Riis Collection, Museum of the City of New York; Kansas State Historical Society
286 Culver; Brown Bros.
287 Brown Bros.
288 California Historical Society; Brown Bros.
289 Granger Collection; California Historical Society
290-291 © David Weintraub
293 Culver
294 Brown Bros.
295 Brown Bros.; Culver
296 Whitney Museum of American Art (Geoffrey Clements)
298 Culver; UPI/Bettmann
299 Mother Cabrini League
300 UPI/Bettmann
301 Henry Ford Museum and Greenfield Village
302 Granger Collection
303 Library of Congress; Culver
304 UPI/Bettmann
306 Bettmann; Bettmann; AP/Wide World
309 Brown Bros.
312 Library of Congress; Chicago Historical Society; University of Chicago Press
313 Dorothea Lange, WRA
315 AP/Wide World

316 AP/Wide World; © J. Barry O'Rourke, The Stock Market
317 Brown Bros.
318 Culver; Reprinted with permission of Joanna T. Steichen. Museum of Modern Art
319 Culver
320 Dorothea Lange, WRA
321 WRA
322 UPI/Bettmann; United Nations; AP/Wide World
323 AP/Wide World
325 UPI/Bettmann
326 Shooting Star
327 © Copyright Academy of Motion Picture Arts and Sciences
329 Shooting Star
330-331 © Joseph Rodriquez, Black Star
332 © Andrew Popper, Picture Group
334 © Dallas and John Heaton, TSW/Chicago; Visual Communications; © J. L. Atlan, Sygma
335 © Dennis Stock, Magnum
336 © P. Zachmann, Magnum
337 © Richard Cash, Photoedit
338 AP/Wide World
339 © Peter LeGrand, TSW/Chicago
340 AP/Wide World
342 Limestone Press; State Russian Museum, Leningrad; State Russian Museum, Leningrad
343 The *Alaska Journal®*; Culver
344 Archives of the Episcopal Church; © Nancy Simmerman, TSW/Chicago; © James, Photo Researchers
345 Brown Bros.; National Portrait Gallery, London; Hawaii State Archives, Honolulu
346 © Nik Wheeler; Bishop Museum; Brown Bros.; Ray Jerome Baker from Robert Van Dyke Collection
347 © Dallas and John Heaton, TSW/Chicago; Kurt Scholz, Shostal
348 © Black Star; © Brent Jones
349 © Matthew Waythons, Black Star; © Joe Cantrelle, Black Star
351 © A. Tannenbaum, Sygma
352 © Magnum
353 © S. Bassouls, Sygma
354 © Simonpietri, Sygma
355 © Philip Jones Griffiths, Magnum
357 © Ira Wyman, Sygma
358 © Randy Taylor, Sygma
359 © Alex Webb, Magnum
360 © *Miami Herald* from Black Star
361 © Alex Webb, Magnum
362 © Bonnie Kamin, Comstock; Copyrighted 1991, Chicago Tribune Company, All Rights Reserved, used with permission; © Levenson, Gamma/Liaison
363 George Ballis, Black Star
364 © Danny Lehaman, After-Image
365 Ra Z. Shakoor; © Robert E. Daemmrich, TSW/Chicago
366 © Phil Huber, Black Star
368 © J. P. Laffont, Sygma
369 © Robert E. Daemmrich, TSW/Chicago
370 © Rohan, TSW/Chicago; © Keith Olson, TSW/Chicago
371 © Dave Bartruff; © Joseph Rodriguez, Black Star
373 © Stuart Cohen, Comstock
374 AP/Wide World
375 Walter Kale, Copyrighted 1991, Chicago Tribune Company, All Rights Reserved, used with permission
376-377 © Robert E. Daemmrich, TSW/Chicago
378 © C. Allan Morgan Space Biospheres Ventures; © Scott McMullen, Space Biospheres Ventures
379 © D. Parrish Snyder, Space Biospheres Ventures; © Sarid, Space Biospheres Ventures

# INDEX

*Note:* Page numbers in italic are references to illustrations.

World Book Encyclopedia, Inc., offers a wide range of educational and reference materials, including the *World Book of America's Presidents*. This two-volume set chronicles the history of the office and the personalities that have filled it. For more information on the *World Book of America's Presidents*, as well as our wide selection of educational and reference books, please write: World Book Encyclopedia, Inc., P.O. Box 3073, Evanston, IL 60204-3073.